interchange

THIRD EDITION

Jack C. Richards
with Jonathan Hull and Susan Proctor

서창국제어학원
WORKBOOK

1

CAMBRIDGE UNIVERSITY PRESS
Cambridge, New York, Melbourne, Madrid, Cape Town, Singapore, São Paulo

Cambridge University Press
40 West 20th Street, New York, NY 10011–4211, USA

www.cambridge.org
Information on this title: www.cambridge.org/9780521601771

First published 2005
2nd printing 2005
Interchange Third Edition Workbook 1 has been developed from *New Interchange* Workbook 1,
first published by Cambridge University Press in 1997.
Printed in Hong Kong, China
Typeface New Century Schoolbook *System* QuarkXPress®

ISBN-13 978-0-521-60177-1 paperback
ISBN-10 0-521-60177-0 paperback

Art direction, book design, photo research, and layout services: Adventure House, NYC

Contents

Acknowledgments

Illustrations

Rob De Bank 7, 48, 90
Tim Foley 52 (*top*)
Travis Foster 16, 70
Jeff Grunewald 17 (*first and fourth columns*)
Randy Jones 1, 9, 12, 21, 36, 46, 47, 49, 51, 52 (*bottom*), 66, 72, 73, 78, 79, 86, 95

Mark Kaufman 13 (*bottom*), 17 (*second, third, and fifth columns*)
Ben Shannon 5, 13 (*top*), 23, 35, 50
Dan Vasconcellos 11, 14, 25, 53, 91, 92
Sam Viviano 2, 3, 15, 42, 54, 69, 77

Photo credits

4 (*clockwise from top left*) © George Ancona/International Stock; © Superstock; © David R. Frazier/Photo Researchers; © Noblestock/International Stock
6 © Fotosearch
8 (*clockwise from upper left*) © Zigy Kaluzny/Getty Images; © Mugshots/Corbis; © Gabe Palmer/Corbis; © Adam Smith/Getty Images; © John Riley/Getty Images
10 (*from top to bottom*) © Frank Herholdt/Getty Images; Phyllis Picardi/International Stock; Larry Gatz/Getty Images
18 (*clockwise from left*) © The Sharper Image 1-800-344-4444; © The Sharper Image 1-800-344-4444; © The Sharper Image 1-800-344-4444; © The Sharp Wizard OZ 5600 electronic organizer
19 (*top to bottom*) © Jennifer Graylock/AP/Wide World Photos; © Tammy Arroyo/AP/Wide World Photos
20 (*clockwise from top left*) © Neal Preston/Corbis; © Mark Seliger/Virgin Records; © Scott McKiernan/Getty Images; © Munawar Hosain/Getty Images; (*bottom*) © Photofest
23 © Warner Brothers Television/Getty Images
24 (*top to bottom*) © Richard Drew/AP/Wide World Photos; © The Everett Collection
26 (*left to right*) © Donald C. Johnson/Corbis; © Alan Smith/Getty Images
27 (*top to bottom*) © Simone Huber/Getty Images; © Anthony Edgeworth/Corbis; © Bill Aron/Photo Researchers; © Dan Bosler/Getty Images; © Graham Harris/Getty Images
30 (*left to right*) © Bill Losh/Getty Images; © Paul Barton/Corbis
31 (*clockwise from top*) © Dave Rosenberg/Getty Images; © Jim Cummins/Getty Images; © Alan Becker/Getty Images
33 © age Fotostock
34 (*clockwise from top left*) © Jean Francois Causse/Getty Images; © Paul Elson/Getty Images; © Dick Dickenson/International Stock
37 © Superstock
38 (*left to right*) © Martin Riedl/Getty Images; © Getty Images
40 © Benjamin Rondel/Corbis
41 (*top to bottom*) © William E. Townsend/Photo Researchers; © Clem Hager/Photo Researchers
55 (*clockwise from left*) © Getty Images; © Masterfile; © Corbis/Sygma

56 © Blair Seitz/Photo Researchers
57 (*clockwise from top left*) © Doug Armand/Getty Images; © Ken Straiton/Corbis; © Ned Gillette/Corbis; © Gary Landsman/Corbis; © Jon Riley/Getty Images; © Viviane Moos/Corbis
59 (*left to right*) © Michael Goldman/Getty Images; © Robert A. Issacs/Photo Researchers; © Hoa-Qui/Getty Images; © Frederick McKinney/Getty Images
60 © Alamy
61 (*top to bottom*) © Will & Deni McIntyre/Getty Images; © Zefa London/Corbis
62 (*left to right*) © Richard Passmore/Getty Images; © EPA/David G. McIntyre/AP/Wide World Photos; © Wonderfile
63 (*top to bottom*) © Joe Cornish/Stone/Getty Images; © Eric Sander/Getty Images
64 (*left to right*) © Gavin Hellier/Getty Images; © Jeffrey Sylvester/Getty Images; © Alexis Duclos/Getty Images
65 © Noboru Komine/Photo Researchers
71 © Bruce Ayers/Getty Images
74 (*top to bottom*) © Matthew Klein/Photo Researchers; © Peter Johansky/Getty Images; © Roy Morsch/Corbis; © Karen Leeds/Corbis; © Alan Bergman/Getty Images
76 (*top to bottom*) © Larry Gatz/Getty Images; © Wonderfile; © Brian Leatart/Foodpix
80 © Travelpix/Getty Images
81 (*left to right*) © Guido Alberto Rossi/Getty Images; © Bob Abraham/Pacific Stock; © A & L Sinibaldi/Getty Images
82 (*top to bottom*) © Dennis Puleston/Photo Researchers; © Robert W. Hernandez/Photo Researchers
83 (*top to bottom*) © Ken Fisher/Getty Images; © Telegraph Colour Library/Getty Images; © Wolfgang Kaehler/Getty Images; © Karl Weidman/Photo Researchers; © Donovan Reese/Getty Images
93 (*left to right*) © L.D. Gordon/Getty Images; © Ariel Skelley/Corbis; © John Henly/Corbis
94 © Superstock
96 © Getty Images

1 Please call me Beth.

1 **Write about yourself.**

My first name is _____ .

My last name is _____ .

Please call me _____ .

I'm from _____ .

2 **Put the words in order to make questions. Then answer the questions.**

1. name   your   what's   last   teacher's

   A: _What's your teacher's last name_ _____ ?

   B: _My teacher's last name is_ _____ .

2. name   your   what's   first   teacher's

   A: _____ ?

   B: _____ .

3. from   your   teacher   where   is

   A: _____ ?

   B: _____ .

4. class   your   how   English   is

   A: _____ ?

   B: _____ .

5. classmates   what   your   are   like

   A: _____ ?

   B: _____ .

3 **Choose the correct responses.**

1. A: Hi, I'm Nicole.

   B: _Oh, hi. I'm Michael._

   - Oh, hi. I'm Michael.
   - What do people call you?

2. A: My name is Young Hoon Park.

   B: _____

   - Nice to meet you, Young Hoon.
   - Let's go and say hello.

3. A: Hello. I'm a new club member.

   B: _____

   - Thanks.
   - Welcome.

4. A: I'm sorry. What's your name again?

   B: _____

   - K-I-N-G.
   - Joe King.

5. A: How do you spell your first name?

   B: _____

   - I'm Antonio.
   - A-N-T-O-N-I-O.

6. A: What do people call you?

   B: _____

   - It's Ken Tanaka.
   - Everyone calls me Ken.

4 **Look at the answers. What are the questions?**

1. Jim: What _'s your first name?_

   Bob: My first name's Bob.

2. Jim: What _____

   Bob: My last name's Hayes.

3. Jim: Who _____

   Bob: That's my wife.

4. Jim: What _____

   Bob: Her name is Rosa.

5. Jim: Where _____

   Bob: She's from Mexico.

6. Jim: Who _____

   Bob: They're my wife's parents.

5 *Choose the correct words.*

1. They're my classmates. ___*Their*___ names are Noriko and Kate. (They / Their)

2. We're students. _____ classroom number is 108-C. (Our / We)

3. Excuse me. What's _____ last name again? (you / your)

4. That's Mr. Kim. _____ is in my class. (He / His)

5. _____ name is Elizabeth. Please call me Liz. (I / My)

6. This is Paul's wife. _____ name is Jennifer. (His / Her)

7. My parents are on vacation. _____ are in Korea. (We / They)

8. I'm from Venice, Italy. _____ is a beautiful city. (It / It's)

6 *Complete this conversation with* **am, are, or is.**

Lisa: Who ___*are*___ the men over there, Amy?

Amy: Oh, they _____ on the volleyball team. Let me introduce you.

Hi, Surachai, this _____ Lisa Neil.

Surachai: Pleased to meet you, Lisa.

Lisa: Nice to meet you, too. Where _____ you from?

Surachai: I _____ from Thailand.

Amy: And this _____ Mario. He _____ from Brazil.

Lisa: Hi, Mario.

A Read these four student biographies. Then complete the chart below.

INTERNATIONAL 🌐 LANGUAGE 🌐 SCHOOL

Every month, we introduce new students to the school. This month, we want to introduce four new students to you. Please say "hello" when you see them in school.

 Mario is in English 101. He is from Cali, Colombia. His first language is Spanish, and he also speaks a little French. He wants to be on the school volleyball team. He says he doesn't play very well, but he wants to learn!

Eileen is in Mario's class. She is from Mozambique, in southern Africa. She speaks Swahili and Portuguese. She is studying English and engineering. She wants to be an engineer. She says she does not play any sports, but she wants to make a lot of new friends in her class.

 Su Yin is in English 102. She is from Taiwan. She says she can write and read English pretty well, but she needs a lot of practice speaking English. Her first language is Chinese. In her free time, she wants to play volleyball on the school team.

Finally, meet Ahmed. He is in English 103. He says he can speak a lot of English, but his writing is very bad! Ahmed is from Luxor in Egypt, and his first language is Arabic. He is a baseball player, and he wants to be on the school baseball team.

Name	Where from?	Languages	Sports?
1. _Mario_			
2. _____	_Mozambique, Africa_		
3. _____		_Chinese and English_	
4. _____			_baseball_

B Write a short biography of a classmate.

_____

_____

_____

_____

Choose the correct sentences to complete this conversation.

> ☐ And what are you studying?
> ☐ No, she's not. She's my sister!
> ☑ Hi, Sarah. I'm Rich. How are you?
> ☐ Oh, really? Is Susan Miller in your class?
> ☐ No, I'm not. I'm on vacation. Are you a student?

Sarah: Hello, I'm Sarah.

Rich: *Hi, Sarah. I'm Rich. How are you?*

Sarah: Pretty good, thanks. Are you a student here?

Rich: _____

Sarah: Yes, I am.

Rich: _____

Sarah: I'm studying Spanish.

Rich: _____

Sarah: Yes, she is. Is she your friend?

Rich: _____

9

Complete this conversation. Use contractions where possible.

> ### Grammar note: Contractions
>
> **Do not use contractions for short answers with Yes.**
> Are you from Argentina?   Is he from Greece?
>   Yes, I am. (*not* Yes, I'm.)   Yes, he is. (*not* Yes, he's.)

Alex: Hello. _____*I'm*_____ Alex Lam.

And this is my sister Amy.

Tina: Hi. _____ Tina Fernandez.

Amy: Are you from South America, Tina?

Tina: Yes, _____ . _____ from Argentina.

Where are you and your sister from, Alex?

Alex: _____ from Taiwan.

Tina: Are you from Taipei?

Alex: No, _____ . _____ from Tainan.

Say, are you in English 101?

Tina: No, _____ . I'm in English 102.

10 *Look at the answers. What are the questions?*

1. A: *Are you on vacation here?*

   B: No, I'm not on vacation. I'm a student here.

2. A: _____

   B: No, I'm not. I'm very busy.

3. A: _____

   B: No, we're not from Spain. We're from Mexico.

4. A: _____

   B: No, my teacher isn't Mr. Brown. I'm in Ms. West's class.

5. A: _____

   B: Yes, Kim and Mika are in my class.

6. A: _____

   B: Yes, it's an interesting class.

7. A: _____

   B: No, they're not on the same baseball team. They're on

   the same volleyball team.

11 *Look at the expressions. Which ones say "hello" and which ones say "good-bye"?*

	Hello	Good-bye
1. How are you doing?	☑	☐
2. See you around.	☐	☐
3. So long.	☐	☐
4. How's everything?	☐	☐
5. Long time, no see.	☐	☐
6. See you Monday.	☐	☐
7. Have a good weekend.	☐	☐
8. Hi there!	☐	☐

12 *Answer these questions about yourself. Use contractions where possible.*

1. Are you from South America? _____

2. Are you on vacation? _____

3. Are you a student at a university? _____

4. Is your English class in the morning? _____

5. Is your teacher from England? _____

6. Is your first name "popular"? _____

2 How do you spend your day?

1 **Match the words in columns A and B. Write the names of the jobs.**

A	B	
☑ company	☐ designer	1. _company director_
☐ computer	☑ director	2. _____
☐ disc	☐ guard	3. _____
☐ fashion	☐ guide	4. _____
☐ security	☐ jockey	5. _____
☐ tour	☐ programmer	6. _____

2 **Write sentences using He or She.**

1. I'm a computer programmer. I work in
   an office. I like computers a lot.
   _He_____

2. I work in a nightclub. I'm a disc jockey.
   I play music.
   _She_____

3. I'm a security guard. I work in a department
   store. I guard the store at night.
   _He_____

4. I work in a design studio. I create beautiful
   fashions. I'm a fashion designer.
   _She_____

7

3 *Write* a *or* an *in the correct places.*

1. He's *a* carpenter. He works for *a* construction company. He builds schools and hospitals.

2. She works for travel company and arranges tours. She's travel agent.

3. He has difficult job. He's cashier. He works in supermarket.

4. She's architect. She works for large company. She builds houses. It's interesting job.

5. She works with computers in office. She's Web-site designer. She's also part-time student. She takes English class in the evening.

4 *Choose someone in your family. Write about his or her job.*

_____

_____

_____

_____

5 Complete this conversation with the correct words.

Tom: What ___does___ your husband _____ exactly?
        (do / does)   (do / does)

Liz: He _____ for a department store. He's a store manager.
        (work / works)

Tom: How _____ he _____ it?
        (do / does)   (like / likes)

Liz: It's an interesting job. He _____ it very much.
                              (like / likes)

But he _____ long hours. And what _____ you _____ ?
       (work / works)   (do / does)   (do / does)

Tom: I'm a student. I _____ architecture.
                      (study / studies)

Liz: Oh, really? Where _____ you _____ to school?
                        (do / does)   (go / goes)

Tom: I _____ to Lincoln University. My girlfriend _____ there, too.
       (go / goes)   (go / goes)

Liz: Really? And what _____ she _____ ?
                       (do / does)   (study / studies)

Tom: She _____ hotel management.
         (study / studies)

Liz: That sounds interesting.

6 Complete the questions in this conversation.

Mark: Where _do you work?_____

Victor: I work for American Express.

Mark: And what _____ there?

Victor: I'm in management.

Mark: How _____

Victor: It's a great job. And what _____

Mark: I'm a salesperson.

Victor: Really? What _____

Mark: I sell computers. Do you want to buy one?

7 *Read these two interviews, and answer the questions.*

Today, *Job Talk* interviews two people with interesting jobs.

Job Talk: Felix, where do you work?

Felix: I work at home, and I work in Southeast Asia.

Job Talk: Really? Well, what do you do at home?

Felix: I'm a chef. I practice cooking new things, and then I write cookbooks.

Job Talk: That sounds interesting. And what do you do in Southeast Asia?

Felix: I make TV programs about Thai cooking.

Job Talk: You have an interesting life, Felix.

Felix: Yes, but it's hard work!

Job Talk: How do you like your job, Julia?

Julia: I love it, but I work long hours.

Job Talk: Do you work late?

Julia: Yes, I work until eight or nine o'clock in the evening. But I take three or four hours for lunch.

Job Talk: Really! But what do you do exactly?

Julia: I stay in all the best new hotels and . . .

Job Talk: Are you a hotel manager?

Julia: No, I'm an electrician! I do the electrical work in new hotels.

1. What does Felix do? _He_ _____

2. What does he do at home? _____

3. What does he do in Southeast Asia? _____

4. What does Julia do? _She_ _____

5. When does she finish work? _____

6. How does she like her job? _____

8 *Meet Pat. Write questions about him using* **What, Where, When,** *and* **How.**

1. _What does he do?_ _____

2. _____

3. _____

4. _____

MERCY HOSPITAL

Patrick Kennedy

Registered Nurse/Night Shift

9 How does Pat spend his weekends? Complete this paragraph with the words from the list.

| ☐ around | ☐ at | ☐ before | ☐ early | ☐ in | ☐ late | ☑ on | ☐ until |

Everyone knows Pat at the hospital. Pat is a part-time nurse. He works at night on weekends. _____On_____ Saturdays and Sundays, Pat sleeps most of the day and wakes up a little _____ nine _____ the evening, usually at 8:45 or 8:50. He has breakfast very late, _____ 9:30 or 10:00 P.M.! He watches television _____ eleven o 'clock, and then starts work _____ midnight. _____ in the morning, usually around 5:00 A.M., he leaves work, has a little snack, goes home, goes to bed, and sleeps _____ . It's a perfect schedule for Pat. He's a pre-med student on weekdays at a local college.

10 Use these words to complete the crossword puzzle.

☐ answers	☐ sells	☐ types
☐ does	☐ serves	☐ works
☐ gets	☑ starts	☐ writes
☐ goes	☐ takes	

Across

1 Lauren _____ work at 5:00 P.M.

4 Karen _____ in a hospital.

5 Ellen _____ up early in the morning.

7 Seoul Garden _____ good Korean food.

9 Rodney _____ to bed after midnight.

10 Andrea is a receptionist. She _____ the phone and greets people.

Down

2 Linda is a tour guide. She _____ people on tours.

3 Dan _____ 100 words a minute on his new computer.

4 Mei-li _____ about 30 e-mails a week.

6 My father works in a bookstore. He _____ books and magazines.

8 What _____ your sister do?

11 **Choose the sentences in the box that have the same meaning as the sentences below.**

- ☐ He goes to the university.
- ☐ She serves food in a restaurant.
- ☐ She stays up late.
- ☐ What does he do?
- ☑ He's an aerobics teacher.
- ☐ He works part time.

1. He teaches aerobics.

   He's an aerobics teacher.

2. Where does he work?

   _____

3. She's a waitress.

   _____

4. He's a student.

   _____

5. She goes to bed at midnight.

   _____

6. He works four hours every day.

   _____

12 **Fill in the missing words or phrases from these job advertisements.**

1. ☐ at night
   ☐ part time
   ☐ weekends
   ☑ nurses

2. ☐ Interesting
   ☐ Spanish
   ☐ tours
   ☐ student

3. ☐ manager
   ☐ long hours
   ☐ restaurant
   ☐ until

New York Hospital needs

_____nurses_____ .

Work during the day or
_____ , weekdays or
_____ , full time
or _____ .

Call 614-555-1191.

_____
job for a language
_____ .

Mornings only. Take people on
_____ . Need good
English and _____ .

Call 917-555-3239.

No need to work
_____ !
Only work from 6:00
_____ 11:00
four evenings a week .
Our _____
serves great food! Work
as our _____ .

Call 308-555-6845.

3 How much is it?

1 **Choose the correct sentences to complete this conversation.**

☐ Which one?
☑ Which ones?
☐ Oh, Sam. Thank you very much.
☐ Well, I like it, but it's expensive.
☐ Yes. But I don't really like light blue.

Sam: Look at those pants, Rebecca.

Rebecca: *Which ones?*

Sam: The light blue ones over there. They're nice.

Rebecca: _____

Sam: Hmm. Well, what about that sweater? It's perfect for you.

Rebecca: _____

Sam: This red one.

Rebecca: _____

Sam: Hey, let me buy it for you. It's a present!

Rebecca: _____

2 **Complete these conversations with How much is / are . . . ?
and this, that, these, or those.**

1. A: *How much is this* _____ backpack?

   B: It's $31.99.

2. A: _____ bracelets?

   B: They're $29.

3. A: _____ shoes?

   B: They're $64.

4. A: _____ dog?

   B: That's *my* dog, and he's not for sale!

3 **Write the plurals of these words.**

> **Spelling note: Plural nouns**
>
> | **Most words** | | **Words ending in -ss, -sh, -ch, and -x** | |
> |---|---|---|---|
> | cap | cap**s** | glass | glass**es** |
> | shoe | shoe**s** | dish | dish**es** |
> | | | watch | watch**es** |
>
> | **Words ending in -f and -fe** | | **Words ending in consonant + -y** | |
> |---|---|---|---|
> | shelf | shel**ves** | country | countr**ies** |
> | knife | kni**ves** | | |

1. backpack _backpacks_   7. necklace _____

2. company _____   8. ring _____

3. dress _____   9. scarf _____

4. day _____   10. sweater _____

5. glove _____   11. tie _____

6. hairbrush _____   12. box _____

4 **What do you think of these prices? Write a response.**

That's cheap.	That's not bad.	That's reasonable.	That's pretty expensive!

1. $90 for a polyester tie

   That's pretty expensive! _____

2. $150 for gold earrings

   _____

3. $500 for a silk dress

   _____

4. $40 for leather gloves

   _____

5. $2,000 for a computer

   _____

6. $5 for two plastic hairbrushes

   _____

7. $15 for a silver necklace

   _____

5 **Choose the correct words to complete the conversations.**

1. Clerk: Good afternoon.

   Luis: Oh, hi. How much is _____*this*_____ watch?
   (this / these)

   Clerk: _____ $195.
   (It's / They're)

   Luis: And how much is that _____ ?
   (one / ones)

   Clerk: _____ $255.
   (It's / They're)

   Luis: Oh, really? Well, thanks, anyway.

2. Kim: Excuse me. How much are _____ jeans?
   (that / those)

   Clerk: _____ only $59.
   (It's / They're)

   Kim: And how much is _____ sweater?
   (this / these)

   Clerk: Which _____ ? They're all different.
   (one / ones)

   Kim: I like this green _____ .
   (one / ones)

   Clerk: _____ $34.
   (It's / They're)

   Kim: Well, that's not bad.

3. Sonia: I like _____ sunglasses over there.
   (that / those)

   Clerk: Which _____ ?
   (one / ones)

   Sonia: The small brown _____ .
   (one / ones)

   Clerk: _____ $199.
   (It's / They're)

   Sonia: Oh, they're expensive!

6 What do you make out of these materials? Complete the chart using words from the list. (You will use words more than once.)

boots   pants   bracelet   ring   gloves   shirt   jacket   necklace

Cotton	Gold	Leather	Silk	Plastic	Wool
pants					

7 Make comparisons using the words given. Add *than* if necessary.

cotton gloves

leather gloves

1. A: These cotton gloves are nice.

   B: Yes, but the leather ones are _____*nicer*_____ . (nice)

   A: They're also _____ . (expensive)

2. A: Those silk jackets look

   _____

   the wool ones. (attractive)

   B: Yes, but the wool ones are

   _____ . (warm)

silk jackets

wool jackets

purple shirt

red shirt

3. A: This purple shirt is an

      interesting color!

   B: Yes, but the color is

      _____ the design. (pretty)

   A: The design isn't bad.

   B: I think the pattern on that red shirt

      is _____ the pattern on

      this purple one. (good)

4. A: Hey, look at this gold ring! It's nice.

      And it's _____ that silver ring. (cheap)

   B: But it's _____ the silver one. (small)

   A: Well, yeah. The silver one is _____ the gold one. (big)

      But look at the price tag. One thousand dollars is a lot of money!

$650.⁰⁰

gold ring

$1,000.⁰⁰

silver ring

8 Complete the chart. Use the words from the list.

☑ athletic shoes	☐ dress	☐ ring
☐ bracelet	☐ earrings	☐ sweater
☐ cap	☐ laptop computer	☐ television
☐ CD player	☐ necklace	☐ video camera

Clothing	Electronics	Jewelry
athletic shoes		

9 Answer these questions. Give your own information.

1	**2**	**3**	**4**	**5**
black sunglasses	wool cap	high-top shoes	laptop computer	19-inch television
white sunglasses	leather cap	tennis shoes	desktop computer	25-inch television

1. Which ones do you prefer, the black sunglasses or the white sunglasses?
   I prefer the black ones.

2. Which cap do you like more, the wool one or the leather one?
   _____

3. Which ones do you like more, the high-tops or the tennis shoes?
   _____

4. Which one do you prefer, the laptop computer or the desktop computer?
   _____

5. Which television do you like better, the 19-inch one or the 25-inch one?
   _____

10 **Great electronic gadgets!**

1 ___

2 ___

3 ___

A Match the ads and the pictures.

a. Find the correct spelling and pronunciation of more than 80,000 words with this electronic dictionary! Made of strong plastic. Comes in two colors – dark gray or light blue. $104.50.

b. Problems with a crossword puzzle? Try this crossword puzzle solver! Simply key in the letters you know and a "?" for the ones you don't know. In seconds, the gadget fills the blanks. Has a database of 130,000 words. Great value at only $49.95.

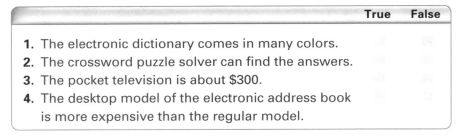

4 ___

c. Watch your favorite baseball game at work or at school! This TV fits in your pocket, only 6" × 1" (15 cm × 2 cm). Gives an excellent picture. Yours for only $299.50.

d. Use the electronic address book for the names and addresses of all your friends. Takes up to 400 names, addresses, and phone numbers. Plastic case included. Regular model $59.95. Desktop model available for $64.95.

B Check (✓) True or False.

	True	False
1. The electronic dictionary comes in many colors.		
2. The crossword puzzle solver can find the answers.		
3. The pocket television is about $300.		
4. The desktop model of the electronic address book is more expensive than the regular model.		

C What's special about an electronic gadget or another item you have? Write a paragraph about it.

_____

_____

_____

_____

_____

_____

4 Do you like rap?

1 Check (✓) the boxes to complete the survey about music and movies.

1 How often do you listen to these types of music?

	Often	Sometimes	Not often
pop	☐	☐	☐
classical	☐	☐	☐
gospel	☐	☐	☐
rock	☐	☐	☐
jazz	☐	☐	☐

2 How often do you watch these types of movies?

	Often	Sometimes	Not often
science fiction	☐	☐	☐
horror films	☐	☐	☐
thrillers	☐	☐	☐
westerns	☐	☐	☐
comedies	☐	☐	☐

2 What do you think of these kinds of entertainment? Answer the questions with the expressions and pronouns in the box.

Yes, I do. I love . . . I like . . . a lot. **No, I don't.** I don't like . . . very much. I can't stand . . .	**Object pronouns** him her it them

Justin Timberlake

Beyoncé Knowles

1. Do you like salsa?

   Yes, I do. I like it a lot.

2. Do you like Justin Timberlake?

   _____

3. Do you like rap?

   _____

4. Do you like Beyoncé Knowles?

   _____

5. Do you like reality TV shows?

   _____

6. Do you like soap operas?

   _____

3 Choose the correct job for each picture.

☐ an actor   ☐ a rock band   ☐ a singer   ☐ a TV talk show host

1. Julio Iglesias is _____

_____

2. The Rolling Stones are _____

_____

3. Oprah Winfrey is _____

_____

4. Matt Damon is _____

_____

4 Complete these conversations.

1.   Ed: ___*Do*___ you ___*like*___ country music, Sarah?

  Sarah: Yes, I _____ it a lot. I'm a real fan of Garth Brooks.

     Ed: Oh, _____ he play the guitar?

  Sarah: Yes, he _____ . He's my favorite musician.

2. Anne: _____ kind of music _____

         your parents _____ , Jason?

  Jason: They _____ classical music.

  Anne: Who _____ they _____ ? Mozart?

  Jason: No, they _____ like him very much. They prefer Beethoven.

3. Scott: Teresa, _____ you _____ Christina Aguilera?

  Teresa: No, I _____ . I can't stand her. I like Pink.

  Scott: I don't know her. What kind of music _____ she sing?

  Teresa: She _____ pop songs. She's really great!

Garth Brooks

5 **Complete these questions and write answers.**

1. _What kinds_ of movies do you like?   _I like_ _____

2. _____ is your favorite movie?   _My favorite_ _____

3. _____ of TV shows do you like?   _____

4. _____ is your favorite TV actor or actress?   _____

5. _____ is your favorite song?   _____

6. _____ is your favorite rock band?   _____

6 **What do you think? Answer the questions.**

1. Which films are funnier, horror films or comedies?

   Comedies are funnier than horror films. _____

2. Which movies are more interesting, musicals or science fiction films?

   _____

3. Which films are scarier, horror films or thrillers?

   _____

4. Which films are more exciting, westerns or crime thrillers?

   _____

7 Verbs and nouns

A Which nouns often go with these verbs? Complete the chart. Use each noun only once.

listen to	play	watch
jazz	_____	_____
_____	_____	_____
_____	_____	_____

- ☐ the piano
- ☐ videos
- ☑ jazz
- ☐ the news
- ☐ music
- ☐ the guitar
- ☐ a film
- ☐ the trumpet
- ☐ CDs

B Write a sentence using each verb in part A.

1. _____
2. _____
3. _____

8 Movie reviews

A Read these movie reviews. Choose a title from the box for each review.

House of Laughs   The Best Man Wins   Ahead of Time   Coming Up for Air

1. _____

What are high school kids like in the future? Do you ever wonder? If so, see this movie! The story is about a group of normal 21st century high school kids. After class one day they find a time machine behind the school. One of the teens sees a button marked "2500" and clicks on it. They immediately travel to the beginning of the 26th century. Do they get back in time for school the next day? Watch and find out. ★★★★

2. _____

There are lots and lots of laughs in this movie. It's about a group of young people in London. They all live in the same house in a suburb far from the city center. The characters come from different countries. They speak different languages, so they often have misunderstandings. The script is very funny and the acting is very good. This movie is like a really good TV soap opera. You'll love it! ★★★★★

3. _____

The action never stops in this movie. Police officer Karen Montana wants to catch Mr. X, a mysterious gold thief. Mr. X is stealing gold from an underwater shipwreck. Before Ms. Montana can catch him, she has to learn how to use diving equipment. But every time she goes underwater, he swims to the surface. Of course, she finally catches him, but not until the final minute of this very long film. ★★

B What kind of movie is each one in part A?

1. ☐ a horror film
   ☐ a science fiction film
   ☐ a historical drama

2. ☐ a travel film
   ☐ a western
   ☐ a comedy

3. ☐ a romantic comedy
   ☐ a crime thriller
   ☐ a documentary

9 *Choose the correct responses.*

1. A: What do you think of *Friends*?

   B: *I'm not a real fan of the show.*

   - How about you?
   - I'm not a real fan of the show.

2. A: Do you like gospel music?

   B: _____

   - I can't stand it.
   - I can't stand them.

3. A: There's a baseball game tonight.

   B: _____

   - Thanks. I'd love to.
   - Great. Let's go.

4. A: Would you like to see a movie this weekend?

   B: _____

   - That sounds great!
   - I don't agree.

the cast of *Friends*

10 *Yes or no?*

A Young Ha is inviting friends to a movie. Do they accept the invitation or not? Check (✓) Yes or No for each response.

Accept?	Yes	No
1. I'd love to. What time does it start?	✓	☐
2. Thanks, but I'm not a real fan of his.	☐	☐
3. That sounds great. Where is it?	☐	☐
4. I'd love to, but I have to work until midnight.	☐	☐
5. Thanks. I'd really like to. When do you want to meet?	☐	☐

B Respond to the invitations.

1. I have tickets to a rap concert on Saturday. Would you like to go?

   _____

2. There's a soccer game tonight. Do you want to go with me?

   _____

3. Britney Spears is performing tomorrow at the stadium. Would you like to see her?

   _____

11 **Choose the correct phrases to complete these conversations.**

1. Robin: _Do you like_____ country music, Kate?
   (Do you like / Would you like)

   Kate: Yes, I do. _____ it a lot.
   (I like / I'd like)

   Robin: There's a Dixie Chicks concert on Friday.

   _____ to go with me?
   (Do you like / Would you like)

   Kate: Yes, _____ . Thanks.
   (I love to / I'd love to)

2. Carlos: There's a French film tonight at 11:00.

   _____ to go?
   (Do you like / Would you like)

   Phil: _____ , but I have to study tonight.
   (I like to / I'd like to)

   Carlos: Well, _____ Brazilian films?
   (do you like / would you like)

   Phil: Yes, _____ . I love them!
   (I do / I would)

   Carlos: There's a great Brazilian movie on TV tomorrow.

   _____ to watch it with me?
   (Do you like / Would you like)

   Phil: _____ . Thanks.
   (I like to / I'd love to)

12 **Rewrite these sentences. Find another way to say each sentence using the words given.**

1. Do you like jazz?

   _What do you think of jazz?_____ (think of)

2. Richard doesn't like classical music.

   _____ (can't stand)

3. I think horror films are great!

   _____ (love)

4. Celia doesn't like country music.

   _____ (be a fan of)

5. Do you want to go to a baseball game?

   _____ (would like)

5 Tell me about your family.

1 **Which words are for males? Which are for females? Complete the chart.**

☑ aunt	☑ brother	☐ daughter	☐ father	☐ husband	☐ mother
☐ nephew	☐ niece	☐ sister	☐ son	☐ uncle	☐ wife

Males	Females
brother ♂ _____	_aunt_ ♀
_____ _____	

2 **Complete this conversation. Use the present continuous of the verbs given.**

Joel: You look tired, Don. _Are you studying_ (study)
late at night these days?

Don: No, I'm not. My brother and sister _____ (stay)
with me right now. We go to bed after midnight every night.

Joel: Really? What _____ (do) this
summer? _____ (take) classes, too?

Don: No, they aren't. My brother is on vacation now, but he
_____ (look) for a part-time job here.

Joel: What about your sister? _____ (work)?

Don: Yes, she is. She has a part-time job at the university.
What about you, Joel? Are you in school this summer?

Joel: Yes, I am. I _____ (study) two languages.

Don: Oh, _____ (take) French and
Spanish again?

Joel: Well, I'm taking Spanish again, but I
_____ (start) Japanese.

Don: Really? That's exciting!

**Rewrite these sentences. Find another way to say each
sentence using the words given.**

1. Joseph is Maria's uncle.

   Maria is Joseph's niece.   (niece)

2. Liz is married to Peter.

   Peter is _____ (husband)

3. Isabel is Frank's and Liza's granddaughter.

   _____ (grandparents)

4. We have two children.

   _____ (son and daughter)

5. My wife's father is a painter.

   _____ (father-in-law)

6. Michael does not have a job right now.

   _____ (look for)

4   **Choose the correct sentences to complete this conversation.**

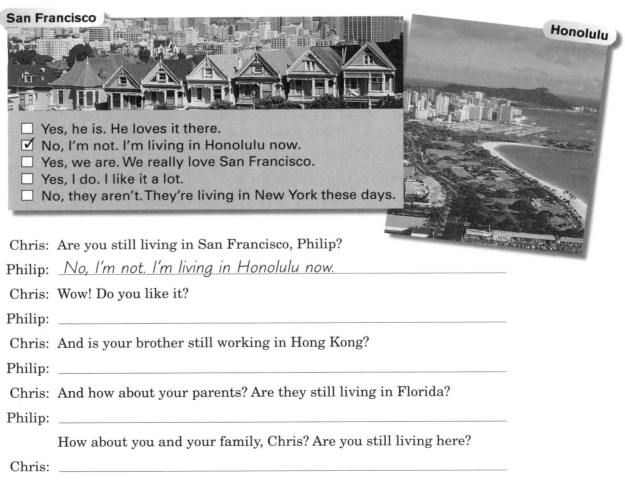

San Francisco

Honolulu

☐ Yes, he is. He loves it there.
☑ No, I'm not. I'm living in Honolulu now.
☐ Yes, we are. We really love San Francisco.
☐ Yes, I do. I like it a lot.
☐ No, they aren't. They're living in New York these days.

Chris: Are you still living in San Francisco, Philip?

Philip: _No, I'm not. I'm living in Honolulu now._

Chris: Wow! Do you like it?

Philip: _____

Chris: And is your brother still working in Hong Kong?

Philip: _____

Chris: And how about your parents? Are they still living in Florida?

Philip: _____

How about you and your family, Chris? Are you still living here?

Chris: _____

5 Complete these sentences. Use the simple present or the present continuous of the verbs given.

1. This is my aunt Barbara.

   She lives _____ (live) in Rome, but

   _____ (visit) Chile this summer.

   _____ (have) a second home there.

2. And these are my parents.

   _____ (work) in London,

   but _____ (visit) my aunt in Chile

   this month.

3. And here you can see my grandparents.

   _____ (live) in New York, but

   _____ (stay) at my parents' house

   in London now.

4. This is my brother-in-law Edward.

   _____ (want) to be a company

   director. _____ (study) business

   in Canada right now.

5. And this is my niece Christina.

   _____ (go) to high school.

   _____ (like) mathematics, but

   she doesn't like English.

6 Choose a friend or family member. Write about him or her using the simple present and present continuous.

_____

_____

_____

_____

A Answer these questions. Then read the passage.

1. At what age do most young people leave their parents' home in your country? _____

2. Do some young people live with their parents after they get married? _____

Leaving Home

Young people leave their parents' homes at different ages in different parts of the world.

In the United States, a lot of college students do not live at home. They often choose to go to college in different cities – away from their parents. At college, many live in university housing. After college, most people prefer to live in their own homes. They often live alone, but some people rent apartments with others.

These people are called *roommates*. By the age of 22, few young people in the United States live with their parents.

Families stay together longer in many Asian countries and cities. In Hong Kong, for example, nearly all university students live with their parents. Rents in the city are very expensive, and few students have the money to pay for their own apartments. Very few young people live alone or become roommates in a shared apartment. Many young people in Hong Kong continue to live with their parents even after they marry.

B Check (✓) True or False. For statements that are false, write the correct information.

In the United States	True	False
1. Very few students live in university housing. _____	☐	☐
2. Some young adults share apartments with roommates. _____	☐	☐
3. Nearly all young adults live with their parents. _____	☐	☐

In Hong Kong	True	False
4. Not many university students live with their parents. _____	☐	☐
5. Few young people live alone. _____	☐	☐
6. Most young married couples have enough money to live in their own apartments. _____	☐	☐

Arrange the quantifiers from the most to the least.

☐ a lot of	☑ no	**1.** *all*	**6.** _____
☐ most	☐ few	**2.** _____	**7.** _____
☐ a few	☐ not many	**3.** _____	**8.** _____
☐ nearly all	☐ many	**4.** _____	**9.** _____
☑ all	☐ some	**5.** _____	**10.** *no*

9

Rewrite these sentences about the United States using the quantifiers given.

1. Sixty-five percent of children start school before the age of five. A hundred percent of children go to school after the age of five.

   ☐ all   ☑ many

   Many children start school before the age of five.
   _____

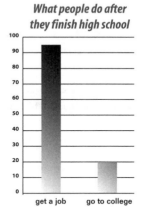

Percentage of children in school by age 5

2. Ninety-five percent of young people get a job after they finish high school. Only 20 percent go to college.

   ☐ nearly all   ☐ a few

   _____
   _____

What people do after they finish high school

3. About 30 percent of people over 65 have part-time jobs. Only about 15 percent like to travel abroad. Fifty-five percent like to stay with their grandchildren.

   ☐ many   ☐ not many   ☐ few

   _____
   _____
   _____

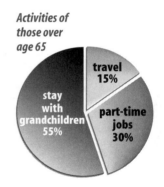

Activities of those over age 65

travel 15%

stay with grandchildren 55%

part-time jobs 30%

10 *Choose the correct words or phrases to complete this paragraph.*

In my country, some _____*couples*_____ (couples / cousins / relatives) get married fairly young. Not many marriages _____ (break up / get divorced / stay together), and nearly all _____ (divorced / married / single) people remarry. Elderly couples often _____ (divorce again / move away / live at home) and take care of their grandchildren.

11 *Complete these sentences about your country. Use the words in the box.*

all	nearly all	most	a lot of	some	few	no

1. _____ young people go to the university.
2. _____ people study English.
3. _____ married couples have more than five children.
4. _____ elderly people have part-time jobs.
5. _____ students have full-time jobs.
6. _____ children go to school on Saturdays.

How often do you exercise?

1 **Complete the chart. Use words from the list.**
(Some of the words can be both individual sports and exercise.)

basketball	baseball	aerobics
yoga	jogging	bicycling
swimming	football	tennis
stretching	soccer	volleyball

team sport

Team sports	Individual sports	Exercise
basketball		

individual sport

exercise

2 *Arrange these words to make sentences or questions.*

1. go   never   I   almost   bicycling
   I almost never go bicycling .

2. hardly   they   tennis   play   ever
   _____ .

3. go   do   often   jogging   how   you
   _____ ?

4. often   mornings   do   on   we   yoga   Sunday
   _____ .

5. ever   Charlie   do   does   aerobics
   _____ ?

6. do   on   you   what   usually   Saturdays   do
   _____ ?

3 Use these questions to complete the conversations.
How often do you . . . ? Do you ever . . . ? What do you usually . . . ?

1. A: _Do you ever exercise?_

   B: Yes, I often exercise on weekends.

2. A: _____

   B: Well, I usually do karate on Saturdays and yoga on Sundays.

3. A: _____

   B: No, I never go to the gym after work.

4. A: _____

   B: I don't exercise very often at all.

5. A: _____

   B: Yes, I sometimes play sports on weekends – usually baseball.

6. A: _____

   B: I usually play tennis in my free time.

4 Keeping fit?

A Check (✓) how often you do each of the things in the chart.

	Every day	Once or twice a week	Sometimes	Not very often	Never
do aerobics	☐	☐	☐	☐	☐
do karate	☐	☐	☐	☐	☐
do weight training	☐	☐	☐	☐	☐
go jogging	☐	☐	☐	☐	☐
go swimming	☐	☐	☐	☐	☐
exercise	☐	☐	☐	☐	☐
play basketball	☐	☐	☐	☐	☐
play soccer	☐	☐	☐	☐	☐

B Write about yourself using the information in the chart.

_____

_____

_____

_____

_____

_____

5 Complete this conversation.
Write the correct prepositions in the correct places.

Susan: What time do you go jogging *in* the morning?   (around / in / on)

 Jerry: I always go jogging 7:00.   (at / for / on)

How about you, Susan?

Susan: I usually go jogging noon.   (around / in / with)

I jog about an hour.   (at / for / until)

 Jerry: And do you also play sports your free time?   (at / in / until)

Susan: No, I usually go out my classmates.   (around / for / with)

What about you?

 Jerry: I go to the gym Mondays and Wednesdays.   (at / on / until)

And sometimes I go bicycling weekends.   (for / in / on)

Susan: Wow! You really like to stay in shape.

6 Complete the crossword puzzle.

Across

4 Pierre never _____ . He's a real couch potato.

6 How often do you _____ yoga?

7 I like to stay in _____ . I play sports every day.

8 Jeff does weight _____ every evening. He lifts weights of 40 kilos.

10 Diana goes _____ for three miles twice a week.

Down

1 Andrew always watches TV in his _____ time.

2 Kate has a regular _____ program.

3 I do _____ at the gym three times a week. The teacher plays great music!

5 Paul is on the _____ team at his high school.

7 Marie never goes _____ when the water is cold.

9 Amy _____ bicycling twice a month.

A Read these ads.

Do you enjoy the outdoors? Do you need exercise? Do you like walking and meeting people?

Join the Hiking Club!
Call 555-1191.

We go on a different hike every weekend. Sometimes we go on a two-day hike and camp overnight!

Adult Education Program at Monroe High School
Mondays to Fridays 6:00-9:00 P.M.

APPLES

la belle pomme

For more information, call 555-6845.

Fall classes: photography; computers for business; typing and word processing; Chinese cooking; Spanish, Portuguese, and Arabic language classes

Come to the YWCA or YMCA! Look at our new activities!
Aerobics, racquetball, softball, yoga!
For anyone from 9 to 90! Singles, couples, and families welcome.
Friday night, teen disco! Saturday night, seniors night!
Phone us at 555-7439.

B Where can you do these activities? Check (✓) the answers.

	Hiking Club	Adult Education Program	YWCA / YMCA
play indoor sports	☐	☐	☐
do outdoor activities	☐	☐	☐
take evening classes	☐	☐	☐
go dancing	☐	☐	☐
learn to cook	☐	☐	☐
meet new people	☐	☐	☐

Choose the correct responses.

1. A: How often do you go swimming, Linda?

   B: _Once a week._

   - I guess I'm OK.
   - Once a week.
   - About an hour.

2. A: How long do you spend in the pool?

   B: _____

   - About 45 minutes.
   - About average.
   - About three miles.

3. A: And how well do you swim?

   B: _____

   - I'm not very well.
   - I almost never do.
   - I'm about average.

4. A: How good are you at other sports?

   B: _____

   - Not very good, actually.
   - I sometimes play twice a week.
   - Pretty well, I guess.

9 **Look at the answers. Write questions using how.**

1. A: _How long do you spend exercising?_

   B: I don't spend any time at all. In fact, I don't exercise.

2. A: _____ for a walk?

   B: Almost every day. I really enjoy it.

3. A: _____

   B: I spend about an hour jogging.

4. A: _____ at soccer?

   B: I'm pretty good at it. I'm on the school team.

5. A: _____

   B: Basketball? Pretty well, I guess. I like it a lot.

10 Rewrite these sentences. Find another way to say each sentence using the words given.

1. I don't watch TV very much.

   I hardly ever watch TV. (hardly ever)

2. Tom exercises twice a month.

   _____ (not very often)

3. Philip tries to keep fit.

   _____ (stay in shape)

4. Jill often exercises at the gym.

   _____ (work out)

5. I go jogging with my wife all the time.

   _____ (always)

6. How good are you at tennis?

   _____ (play)

11 What do you think about sports? Answer these questions.

1. Do you like to exercise for a short time or a long time?

   _____

2. Do you prefer exercising in the morning or in the evening?

   _____

3. Which do you like better, walking or jogging?

   _____

4. Do you like to watch sports or play sports?

   _____

5. Which do you like better, team sports or individual sports?

   _____

6. How good are you at games like basketball or tennis?

   _____

7. What sport or game don't you like?

   _____

7 We had a great time!

1 Past tense

A Write the simple past of these regular verbs.

1. cook _cooked_   4. love _____   7. visit _____

2. enjoy _____   5. study _____   8. wash _____

3. invite _____   6. try _____   9. watch _____

B Write the simple form of these irregular simple past verbs.

1. _buy_   bought   5. _____ slept

2. _____ gave   6. _____ spent

3. _____ met   7. _____ took

4. _____ saw   8. _____ went

C Use two of the verbs above and write sentences about the past.

Example: _We went to a rock concert last night._

1. _____

2. _____

2 Use the cues to answer these questions.

1. Where did you go this weekend?

   I went to a party.   (to a party)

2. Who did you meet at the party?

   _____ (someone very interesting)

3. What time did you and Eva get home?

   _____ (a little after 1:00)

4. How did you and Bob like the art exhibition?

   _____ (a lot)

5. What did you buy?

   _____ (the new Madonna CD)

6. Where did Jeff and Joyce spend their vacation?

   _____ (in the country)

3 *What do you like to do alone? with other people? Complete the chart with activities from the list. Then add one more activity to each list.*

watch TV
read the newspaper
go shopping
do homework
exercise
have a picnic
go to a sports event
cook dinner
take a vacation
go to the movies

Activities I like to do alone	Activities I like to do with other people

4 *Complete the questions in this conversation.*

A: How *did you spend your weekend?*

B: I spent the weekend with Joe and Kathy.

A: What _____

B: Well, on Saturday, we went shopping.

A: And _____ in the evening?

B: No, nothing special.

A: Where _____ on Sunday?

B: We went to the amusement park.

A: How _____

B: We had a great time. In fact, we stayed there all day.

A: Really? What time _____

B: We got home very late, around midnight.

5 **Answer these questions with negative statements. Then add a positive statement using the information below.**

☑ have a boring time   ☐ finish our homework on Saturday   ☐ go out with friends
☐ watch it on TV   ☐ work all day until six o'clock   ☐ take the bus

1. A: We had a great time at Carrie's party. Did you and Jane enjoy it?

   B: *No, we didn't. We had a boring time.*

2. A: I stayed home from work all day yesterday. Did you take the day off, too?

   B: _____

3. A: I worked all weekend on my research paper. Did you spend the weekend at home, too?

   B: _____

4. A: I studied all weekend. Did you and John have a lot of homework, too?

   B: _____

5. A: Carl drove me to work yesterday morning. Did you drive to work?

   B: _____

6. A: Kathy went to the baseball game last night. Did you and Bob go to the game?

   B: _____

6 **Read about Andy's week. Match the sentences that have a similar meaning.**

A	B
1. He was broke last week. ___*f*___	**a.** He had people over.
2. He didn't work on Friday. _____	**b.** He had a good time.
3. He worked around the house. _____	**c.** He didn't do the laundry.
4. He didn't wash the clothes. _____	**d.** He took a day off.
5. He invited friends for dinner. _____	**e.** He did housework.
6. He had a lot of fun. _____	✓ **f.** He spent all his money.

7 Did we take the same trip?

A Do you ever take summer vacations? What kind of vacations do you like to take: relaxing? educational? exciting?

B Read these reports about Thailand.

a temple in Bangkok, Thailand

William's report

We went to Thailand for our summer vacation last year. It was our first trip to Asia. We loved it! We spent a week in Bangkok and did something different every day. We went to the floating market very early one morning. We didn't buy anything there — we just looked. Another day, we went to Wat Phra Keo, the famous Temple of the Emerald Buddha. It was really interesting. Then we saw two more temples nearby. We also went on a river trip somewhere outside Bangkok. The best thing about the trip was the food. The next time we have friends over for dinner, I'm going to cook Thai food.

Sue's report

Last summer, we spent our vacation in Thailand. We were very excited — it was our first trip there. We spent two days in Bangkok. Of course, we got a river taxi to the floating market. We bought some delicious fruit there. The next day we went to a very interesting temple called the Temple of the Emerald Buddha. We didn't have time to visit any other temples. However, we went to two historic cities — Ayuthaya and Sukhothai. Both have really interesting ruins. Everything was great. It's impossible to say what was the best thing about the trip.

C Who did these things on their trip? Check (✓) the answers.

	William	Sue
1. visited Thailand for the first time	☑	☑
2. stayed for two days in Bangkok	☐	☐
3. visited the floating market	☐	☐
4. bought fruit	☐	☐
5. saw some historic ruins	☐	☐
6. traveled on the river	☐	☐
7. loved the food the most	☐	☐
8. enjoyed everything	☐	☐

8 Complete this conversation with *was, wasn't, were,* or *weren't.*

A: How _____*was*_____ your vacation in Peru, Julia?

B: It _____ great. I really enjoyed it.

A: How long _____ you there?

B: We _____ there for two weeks.

A: _____ you in Lima all the time?

B: No, we _____ . We _____ in the mountains
for a few days.

A: And how _____ the weather? _____ it good?

B: No, it _____ good at all. The city _____
very hot, and the mountains _____ really cold!

9 Choose the correct questions to complete this conversation.

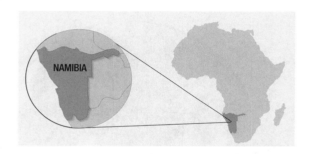

Namibian meerkats

☐ And what was the best part?
☐ How long were you in South Africa?
☑ How was your vacation in Africa?
☐ And how long were you in Namibia?
☐ How was the weather?

A: _How was your vacation in Africa?_____

B: It was a great trip. I really enjoyed South Africa and Namibia.

A: _____

B: For ten days.

A: _____

B: I was in Namibia for about five days.

A: Wow, that's a long time! _____

B: It was hot and sunny the whole time.

A: _____

B: It was definitely the national parks and wildlife in Namibia. And we saw
some meerkats!

10 Choose the correct words or phrases.

1. I'm sorry I was late. I had to _____ a phone call. (do / make / go)

2. My friends and I really enjoyed your party. We all had a _____ time.
   (boring / good / funny)

3. I _____ some photocopies of the report and put them on your desk.
   (did / went / made)

4. We didn't see very much in the mountains. The weather was very _____.
   (cool / foggy / sunny)

5. I worked very hard in Switzerland last week. I was there _____ .
   (in my car / on business / on vacation)

11 My kind of vacation

A What do you like to do on vacation? Rank these
activities from 1 (you like it the most) to
6 (you like it the least).

___ go to the beach

___ look at historical buildings

___ go shopping

___ visit museums

___ spend time at home

___ have good food

B Answer these questions about vacations.

1. How often do you go on vacation?

   _____

2. How long do you spend on vacation?

   _____

3. Who do you usually go with?

   _____

4. Where do you usually go?

   _____

5. What do you usually do on vacation?

   _____

8 What's your neighborhood like?

1 Places

A Match the words in columns A and B. Write the names of the places.

A	B	
☑ barber	☐ agency	1. _barber shop_
☐ gas	☐ bar	2. _____
☐ grocery	☐ café	3. _____
☐ Internet	☐ office	4. _____
☐ karaoke	☐ phone	5. _____
☐ movie	☑ shop	6. _____
☐ pay	☐ station	7. _____
☐ post	☐ store	8. _____
☐ travel	☐ theater	9. _____

B Write questions with "Is there a . . . ?" or "Are there any . . . ?" and the names of places from part A.

1. A: I need a haircut. _Is there a barbershop_ _____ near here?

   B: Yes, there's one on Elm Street.

2. A: I want to send an e-mail. _____ near here?

   B: No, there aren't, but there are some near the university.

3. A: I want to send this letter. _____ around here?

   B: Yes, there's one next to the laundromat.

4. A: I need to make a phone call. _____ around here?

   B: Yes, there are some across from the library.

5. A: We need some gas. _____ on this street?

   B: No, there aren't, but there are a couple on Second Avenue.

6. A: We need to make a reservation for a trip. _____

   near here?

   B: Yes, there's one near the Prince Hotel.

2 **Look at these street maps of Avery and Bailey. There are ten differences between them. Find the other eight.**

> **Grammar note: There are; some *and* any**
>
> **Positive statement**
> There **are some** pay phones near the bank.
>
> **Negative statement**
> There **aren't any** pay phones near the bank.

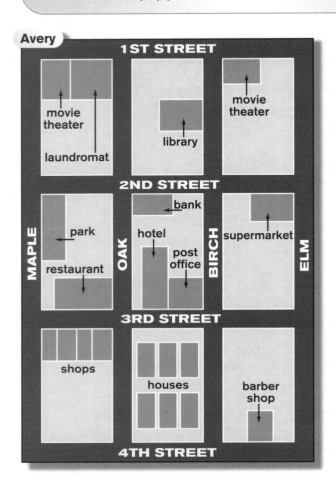

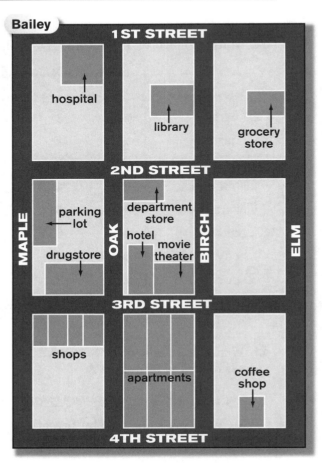

1. _There are some movie theaters on 1st Street in Avery, but there aren't any in Bailey._
2. _There's a park on the corner of 2nd Street and Maple in Avery, but there isn't one in Bailey. There's a parking lot._
3. _____
4. _____
5. _____
6. _____
7. _____
8. _____
9. _____
10. _____

3 **Answer these questions. Use the map and the expressions in the box.**

☐ between ☐ in front of ☐ near
☑ next to ☐ on the corner of ☐ opposite

KING STREET

grocery store
hotel
bank   movie theater

PALM STREET

drugstore   gas station
library
A B C

LINCOLN STREET

laundromat   D
post office

YMCA →

RIVER STREET

1ST AVENUE   2ND AVENUE   3RD AVENUE

A = travel agency   C = gym
B = department store   D = pay phones

1. Where's the nearest bank?
   There's one next to the grocery store on 1st Avenue.

2. Is there a post office near here?
   Yes. There _____

   _____

3. I'm looking for a drugstore.

   _____

   _____

4. Is there a laundromat in this neighborhood?

   _____

   _____

5. Is there a department store on Lincoln Street?

   _____

   _____

6. Are there any pay phones around here?

   _____

   _____

4 **Answer these questions about your city or neighborhood.**
Use the expressions in the box and your own information.

Yes, there is. There's one on . . .   Yes, there are. There are some on . . .
No, there isn't.   No, there aren't.

1. Are there any good restaurants around school?

   _____

2. Is there a police station near school?

   _____

3. Are there any good music stores in your neighborhood?

   _____

4. Is there a karaoke bar close to your home?

   _____

A Read these interviews.

MODERN LIFE

Modern Life magazine asked two people about their neighborhoods.

Interview with Diana Towne

"My neighborhood is very convenient – it's near the shopping center and the bus station. It's also safe. But those are the only good things about living downtown. It's very noisy because the streets are always full of people! The traffic is terrible, and parking is a big problem! I can never park on my own street. I'd like to live in the suburbs."

Interview with Victor Bord

"My wife and I live in the suburbs, and it's just too quiet! There aren't many shops, and there are certainly no clubs or theaters. There are a lot of parks, good schools, and very little crime, but nothing ever really happens here. I would really love to live downtown."

B How do Diana and Victor feel about their neighborhoods? Complete the chart.

	Advantages	**Disadvantages**
Downtown	*near the shopping center*	
Suburbs		

C How do you feel about your neighborhood? Write about it.

_____

_____

_____

_____

6 Complete the chart. Use words from the list.

☑ bank ☐ hospital ☐ noise ☐ people ☐ school ☐ traffic
☑ crime ☐ library ☐ parking ☐ pollution ☐ theater ☐ water

Count nouns		Noncount nouns	
bank	_____	crime	_____
_____	_____	_____	_____
_____	_____	_____	_____

7 Write questions using "How much . . . ?" or "How many . . . ?" Then look at the picture and write answers to the questions. Use the expressions in the box.

☑ a lot ☐ a couple ☐ many ☐ only a little ☐ not any ☐ a lot

1. (noise)   How much noise is there?   _____   There's a lot.   _____
2. (buses)   _____   _____
3. (traffic)   _____   _____
4. (banks)   _____   _____
5. (people)   _____   _____
6. (crime)   _____   _____

8 **Choose the correct words or phrases to complete this conversation.**

Luis: Are there ____*any*____ (any / one / none) nightclubs around here, Alex?

Alex: Sure. There are _____ (any / one / a lot).

There's a great club _____ (across from / between / on)

the National Bank, but it's expensive.

Luis: Well, are there _____ (any / none / one) others?

Alex: Yeah, there are _____ (a few / a little / one).

There's a nice _____ (any / one / some) near here.

It's called Sounds of Brazil.

Luis: That's perfect! Where is it exactly?

Alex: It's on Third Avenue, _____ (between / on / on the corner of)

the Royal Theater and May's Restaurant.

Luis: So let's go!

9 **Choose the correct words or phrases.**

1. I'm going to the stationery store to get some _____ .
   (birthday cards / coffee / food)

2. We're taking a long drive. We need to go to the _____ .
   (laundromat / gas station / travel agency)

3. I live on the 8th floor of my _____ .
   (apartment building / neighborhood / theater)

4. Our apartment is in the center of the city. We live _____ .
   (downtown / in the neighborhood / in the suburbs)

9 What does she look like?

1 **Write the opposites. Use the words in the box.**

☐ light   ☑ straight   ☐ young   ☐ short   ☐ tall

1. curly / _straight_ _____
2. dark / _____
3. elderly / _____

4. long / _____
5. short / _____

2 **Descriptions**

A Match the words in columns A and B. Write the descriptions.

A	B	
☑ dark	☐ aged	**1.** _dark brown_
☐ fairly	☑ brown	**2.** _____
☐ good	☐ height	**3.** _____
☐ medium	☐ long	**4.** _____
☐ middle	☐ looking	**5.** _____

B Answer the questions using the descriptions from part A.

1. A: What does he look like?

   B: _He's good-looking._ _____

2. A: How long is his hair?

   B: _____

3. A: What color is his hair?

   B: _____

4. A: How old is he?

   B: _____

5. A: How tall is he?

   B: _____

3 Complete this conversation with questions.

Steve: Let's find Amy. I need to talk to her.

Jim: *What does she look like?*

Steve: She's quite pretty, with straight black hair.

Jim: And _____

Steve: It's medium length.

Jim: _____

Steve: She's fairly tall.

Jim: And _____

Steve: She's in her early twenties.

Jim: _____

Steve: Sometimes. I think she's wearing them now.

Jim: I think I see her over there. Is that her?

4 Describe yourself. How old are you? What do you look like? What are you wearing today?

_____

_____

_____

_____

_____

5 **Circle two things in each description that do not match the picture. Then correct the information.**

George

1. George is in his (late sixties). He's pretty tall. He has a mustache, and he's bald. He's wearing a shirt, jeans, and boots.

   He isn't in his late sixties. He's in his twenties.

   _____

   _____

   _____

Sophie

2. Sophie is about 25. She's very pretty. She's medium height. Her hair is long and blond. She's wearing a black sweater, a jacket, and tennis shoes. She's standing next to her motorcycle.

   _____

   _____

   _____

   _____

Lucinda

3. Lucinda is in her early twenties. She's pretty serious-looking. She has glasses. She's fairly tall, and has curly dark hair. She's wearing a nice-looking jacket and jeans.

   _____

   _____

   _____

   _____

6 *Which of these clothing items are more formal? Which are more casual? Complete the chart.*

scarf

boots

necktie

skirt

shirt

Formal	Casual
shirt	

T-shirt

dress

suit

shorts

cap

running shoes

jeans

7 *Write a sentence about each person. Use the words in the box and participles.*

Mandy

Edward and Kate

William

Giorgio   Alice

☑ man   ☐ carry a jacket
☐ woman   ☐ wear sunglasses
☐ one   ☑ stand next to Alice
☐ ones   ☐ talk to the man
☐ tall woman   ☐ wear a suit and tie

1. *Giorgio is the man standing next to Alice.*

2. _____

3. _____

4. _____

5. _____

8 Answer the questions. Use the words given.

Ken Carlos Jake Marie Dan Cindy Angela

1. A: Which ones are Jake and Marie?

   B: _They're the ones playing cards._ (playing cards)

2. A: Who's Carlos?

   B: _____ (couch)

3. A: Who are Dan and Cindy?

   B: _____ (dancing)

4. A: Which one is Angela?

   B: _____ (couch)

5. A: Who's Ken?

   B: _____ (short black hair)

9 Rewrite these sentences and questions.
Find another way to say them using the words given.

1. A: Who's Mika?

   Which one's Mika? (Which)

   B: She's the one in the black dress.

   She's the one wearing the black dress. (wearing)

2. A: Which ones are the teachers?

   _____ (Who)

   B: They're the ones on the couch.

   _____ (sitting)

3. A: Which one is Larry?

   _____ (Who)

   B: He's the guy wearing the coat.

   _____ (in)

What does she look like? • 53

10

Complete this description. Use the present continuous or the participle of the verbs in the box.

☐ ask   ☐ carry   ☑ look   ☐ stand   ☐ use   ☐ wait   ☐ walk   ☐ wear

Yeah, classes start tomorrow. What am I doing? Let's see . . . .
I *'m looking* _____ out my window right now.
There's a middle-aged woman _____ her dog,
and a young guy _____ the pay phone. Two people
_____ next to him. Hey! The one _____
a baseball hat is my classmate! Some people _____ at the
bus stop. A serious-looking woman _____ for directions.
And hey, here comes a really cute girl _____ a
backpack. Wait a minute! I know her. That's my old
girlfriend. I have to go now! Bye.

11

Choose the correct responses.

1. A: Where's Jan?

   B: _She couldn't make it._

   - I'd like to meet her.
   - She couldn't make it.

2. A: Who's Sam?

   B: _____

   - I'm afraid I missed him.
   - The handsome guy near the door.

3. A: Is she the one on the couch?

   B: _____

   - That's right.
   - Let's see.

4. A: How tall is she?

   B: _____

   - Fairly long.
   - Pretty short.

10 Have you ever ridden a camel?

1 Match the verb forms in columns A and B.

A	B
1. be <u>d</u>	a. gone
2. call ____	b. done
3. do ____	c. seen
4. eat ____	✓ d. been
5. go ____	e. called
6. have ____	f. jogged
7. jog ____	g. made
8. make ____	h. had
9. see ____	i. tried
10. try ____	j. eaten

2 Complete the questions in these conversations.
Use the present perfect of the verbs in Exercise 1.

1. A: *Have you seen* the new Keanu Reeves movie?

   B: Yes, it's very good.

2. A: _____ running lately?

   B: Yes, Sue usually runs in the morning and evening.

3. A: How many phone calls _____ lately?

   B: I made only one – on my father's birthday.

4. A: How long _____ those sunglasses?

   B: I've had them for a few weeks.

5. A: _____ at Rio Café?

   B: Yes, we've already eaten there. It's very good but
   a little expensive.

6. A: How many times _____ shopping
   at the mall this month?

   B: Actually, I haven't gone at all. Why don't we go
   later today?

Keanu Reeves

3 Already *and* yet

A Check (✓) the things you've done. Put an ✗ next to the things you haven't done.

1. _____ graduated from high school

2. _____ opened an e-mail account

3. _____ gone abroad

4. _____ been in an airplane

5. _____ tried skiing

6. _____ gotten married

> getting married

B Write sentences about each thing in part A. Use *already* and *yet*.

> **Grammar note: Already *and* yet**
>
> **Already *is used in positive statements with the present perfect.***
> I've **already** graduated from high school.
>
> **Yet *is used in negative statements with the present perfect.***
> I haven't graduated from college **yet**.

1. _____

2. _____

3. _____

4. _____

5. _____

6. _____

4 *Complete these sentences with* for *or* since.

1. Damien has lived in Hong Kong _____ 2001.

2. I have been a nurse _____ several years.

3. Masayuki was an exchange student in Spain _____ a whole semester.

4. I'm so sleepy. I've been awake _____ 4:00 this morning.

5. Mr. and Mrs. Chang have been married _____ nearly 40 years.

6. Maggie has had the same hairstyle _____ high school.

7. How are you? I haven't seen you _____ your wedding.

8. Where have you been? I've been here _____ over an hour!

9. I haven't had this much fun _____ I was a kid.

5 *Look at these pictures. How often have you done these things?*
Write sentences using the expressions in the box.

> I've . . . many times
> I've . . . three or four times.
> I've . . . several times.
>
> I've . . . once or twice.
> I haven't . . . lately.
> I've never . . .

ride a roller coaster

1. _____

go to a nightclub

2. _____

go bungee jumping

3. _____

call home

4. _____

see an opera

5. _____

play tennis

6. _____

A Read these stories about two terrible days.

1

NO WAY UP!

Have you ever been in a cable car? Well, I have. Last February, I went on a ski trip to Switzerland. What a trip! The first morning, I got into a cable car. I wanted to go to the top of the mountain and ski down. The cable car started up the mountain. I looked down, and it was so beautiful. Then there was a terrible noise. Suddenly the car stopped. It didn't move, and there was quiet everywhere.

It was cold, and it began to get dark and snow. I was alone for one hour, two hours. I thought, "They've forgotten me!" At last the car started back down the mountain. It went very fast. "Sorry," a man said when I climbed out of the car. "We've never had this problem before. Please, try again tomorrow." "He's joking," I thought. "I've had enough of cable cars for a lifetime."

2

NO WAY OUT!

I have always wanted to go fishing. Last summer, I went on a trip to Taiwan. On the last day of my vacation, I went fishing on a beautiful lake. Unfortunately, I didn't catch any fish, and I got bored. I decided to go swimming. When I stood up, my wallet fell out of the boat and into the water. It had all my money, my passport, my plane tickets – everything! I jumped into the lake to look for it, but I didn't find anything.

The next morning, I wasn't able to leave the hotel. I had no money to pay the bill and no plane ticket or passport to go home. So what did I do? I called my parents and asked for some money. I have never had such a terrible experience!

B In which story or stories did the writer(s) do these things? Write *1*, *2*, or *1 and 2*.

_1_	stayed in the mountains	_____	spent time on a boat
_____	lost a wallet	_____	waited for help
_____	enjoyed the view	_____	went swimming
_____	got no exercise	_____	had a terrible day

C Write about a terrible day you have had. What happened? What went wrong?

_____

_____

_____

_____

_____

7 **Look at the answers. Write questions using Have you ever . . . ?**

 flamenco dancing  sumo wrestlers  oysters  wall climbing

1. A: _Have you ever watched flamenco dancing?_ _____

   B: Yes, I have. I watched flamenco dancing last summer in Spain.

2. A: _____

   B: Actually, I saw a sumo wrestling match last month on TV. It was terrific!

3. A: _____

   B: No, I haven't. I've never eaten oysters.

4. A: _____

   B: Yes, I went wall climbing on Friday night.

5. A: _____

   B: No, I haven't. I've never been camping.

6. A: _____

   B: Yes, I have. I once rode my brother's motorcycle.

7. A: _____

   B: No, I've never been to India.

8 **Write your own answers to the questions in Exercise 7.
Use expressions like the ones from the list.**

Yes I have. I . . . yesterday.	No, I haven't. I've never . . .
I . . . on Monday.	I . . . yet.
I . . . last year.	
I . . . in August.	

1. _____

2. _____

3. _____

4. _____

5. _____

6. _____

7. _____

9 *Complete the conversation. Use the simple past or the present perfect of the words given.*

A: _____ *Have* _____ you ever _____ *lost* _____
(lose) anything valuable?

B: Yes, I _____ (lose) my cell phone last month.

A: _____ you _____
(find) it yet?

B: No. Actually, I _____ already
_____ (buy) a new one. Look!

A: Oh, that's nice. Where _____ you
_____ (buy) it?

B: I _____ (get) it at Tech Town last
weekend. What about you? _____ you
ever _____ (lose) anything valuable?

A: Well, I _____ (leave) my electronic address
book in a coffee shop a couple of months ago.

B: How annoying! Maybe that's why you _____
(not call) me for a while.

A: But you _____ (not call) me in a long time.
What's your excuse?

B: I told you. I _____ (lose) my cell phone!

10 *Choose the correct responses.*

1. A: Has Marie called her family lately?
   B: *No, she hasn't.* _____
   - How many times?
   - No, she hasn't.

2. A: Are you having a good time?
   B: _____
   - Yes, in a long time.
   - Yes, really good.

3. A: How long did Joe stay at the party?
   B: _____
   - For two hours.
   - Since midnight.

4. A: How many times has Gina lost her keys?
   B: _____
   - Twice.
   - Already.

5. A: What about a tour of the city?
   B: _____
   - I've never, have you?
   - Sure. I hear it's great.

6. A: Have you been here long?
   B: _____
   - No, not yet.
   - No, just a few minutes.

11 It's a very exciting place!

1 *Choose the correct words to complete the sentences.*

1. Prices are very high in New York City. Everything is pretty _____*expensive*_____ there.
   (cheap / expensive / stressful)

2. Rome is a beautiful old city. There are not many _____ buildings.
   (big / modern / small)

3. My hometown is not an exciting place. The nightlife there is pretty _____ .
   (boring / nice / interesting)

4. Some parts of our city are fairly dangerous. They're not very _____ late at night.
   (hot / interesting / safe)

5. Athens is a very quiet city in the winter. The streets are never _____ at that time of the year.
   (spacious / crowded / relaxing)

2 *Choose the correct questions to complete this conversation.*

☐ What's the weather like?
☐ Is it big?
☐ Is the nightlife exciting?
☐ What's your hometown like?

A: _____

B: My hometown? It's a pretty nice place and the people are very friendly.

A: _____

B: No, it's fairly small, but it's not *too* small.

A: _____

B: The winter is wet and really cold. It's very nice in the summer, though.

A: _____

B: No! It's really boring. There are no good restaurants or nightclubs.

3 *Choose the correct conjunctions and rewrite the sentences.*

> **Grammar note: And, but, though, *and* however**
>
> **Use and *for additional information.***
> It's an exciting city, **and** the weather is great.
>
> **Use but, though, *and* however *for contrasting information.***
> It's very safe during the day, **but** it's pretty dangerous at night.
> The summers are hot. The evenings are fairly cold, **though**.
> It is a fairly large city. It's not too interesting, **however**.

 **Paris, France**

 **Sapporo, Japan**

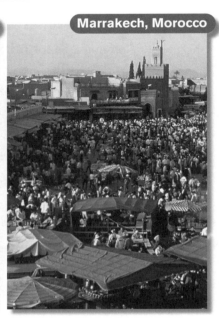 **Marrakech, Morocco**

1. Paris is a very busy place. The streets are always crowded. (and / but)

   Paris is a very busy place, and the streets are always crowded.

   _____

2. Sapporo is a very nice place. The winters are terribly cold. (and / though)

   _____

   _____

3. Marrakech is an exciting city. It's a fun place to sightsee. (and / however)

   _____

   _____

4. My hometown is a great place for a vacation. It's not too good for shopping. (and / but)

   _____

   _____

5. Our hometown is somewhat ugly. It has some beautiful old homes. (and / however)

   _____

   _____

4 **Check (✓) if these sentences need a or an. Then write a or an in the correct places.**

> **Grammar note: A and an**
>
> *Use* **a** *or* **an** *with (adverb +) adjective + singular noun.*
> It has **a fairly new park**.
> It's **an old city**.
>
> *Don't use* **a** *or* **an** *with (adverb +) adjective.*
> It's **fairly new**.
> It's **old**.

Denver International Airport

1. ✓ Denver has ⟨a⟩ very modern airport.
2. ☐ Restaurants are very cheap in Mexico.
3. ☐ Copenhagen is clean city.
4. ☐ The buildings in Paris are really beautiful.
5. ☐ Apartments are very expensive in Hong Kong.
6. ☐ Amsterdam is fairly crowded city in the summer.
7. ☐ Toronto has good museums.
8. ☐ Rio de Janeiro is exciting place to visit.

5 **Complete this description of London with is or has.**

Ever-Popular

London

London ____is____ Britain's biggest city. It _____ a very old capital and dates back to the Romans. It _____ a city of interesting buildings and churches, and it _____ many beautiful parks. It also _____ some of the best museums in the world. London _____ very crowded in the summer, but it _____ not too busy in the winter. It _____ a popular city with foreign tourists and _____ millions of visitors a year. The city _____ famous for its shopping and _____ many excellent department stores. London _____ convenient trains and buses that cross the city, so it _____ easy for tourists to get around.

A Read about these cities.

For many centuries, Budapest was two cities, with Buda on the west side of the Danube River and Pest on the east side. Budapest became one city in 1872, and it has been the capital city of Hungary ever since.

The population of Budapest is about two million, and the city is a very popular place for tourists. Visitors like to take boat rides along the Danube. Budapest is also known for its exciting nightlife. The best time to visit is the summer since Budapest is very cold in the winter.

Los Angeles was founded in 1781. With 3.8 million people, it is now the biggest city in California and the second largest city in the United States. It is famous for its modern freeways, its movie stars, and its smog. When the city is really smoggy, you can't see the nearby mountains. The weather is usually dry and warm.

Visitors like to go to the film studios and to drive along Hollywood Boulevard. There are some good beaches near the city, and Los Angeles is also close to Disneyland.

Since its founding in the eighteenth century, Taipei has grown to a population of 2.7 million and has become the cultural, industrial, and administrative center of the island of Taiwan. It's an exciting city, but the weather is humid and not always pleasant.

Taipei is also a busy city, and the streets are always full of people. There is an excellent museum that many tourists visit. It's a fairly expensive city, but not more expensive than some other Asian cities, so many tourists go to Taipei to shop.

B Complete the chart.

City	Date founded	Population	Weather	Attractions
Budapest	*1872*			
Los Angeles				
Taipei				

C Complete the sentences

1. *Taipei* _____ is cheaper than some other cities nearby.
2. _____ has good beaches nearby.
3. _____ was once two cities.
4. _____ were both founded in the eighteenth century.

7 Complete these sentences. Use phrases from the list.

☐ shouldn't miss   ☐ can take
☑ should see   ☐ shouldn't stay
☐ should get around   ☐ shouldn't walk

1. You *should see* the new zoo.
   It's very interesting.

2. You _____ near the
   airport. It's too noisy.

3. You _____ the museum.
   It has some new exhibits.

4. You _____ a bus tour
   of the city if you like.

5. You _____ alone at night.
   It's too dangerous.

6. You _____ by taxi if
   you're out late.

8 Complete this conversation with should or shouldn't and I or you.

A: I'm taking my vacation in Indonesia.
     What *should I* do there?

B: _____ miss Jogjakarta,
     the old capital city. There are a lot of
     beautiful old buildings. For example,
     _____ see the
     temple of Borobudur.

A: Sounds great. Bali is very popular, too.
     _____ go there?

B: Yes, _____ .
     It's very interesting.

A: _____ take a lot of
     money with me?

B: No, _____ . Indonesia
     is not an expensive country to visit.

A: So when _____ go there?

B: Anytime. The weather's always nice.

Jogjakarta, Indonesia

9 **Ask questions about a place you want to visit.
Use** can, should, *or* shouldn't.

1. the time to visit

   What time of year should you visit?

2. things to see and do there

   _____

3. things not to do

   _____

4. special foods to try

   _____

5. fun things to buy

   _____

6. other interesting things to do

   _____

10 **Rewrite these sentences. Find another way to say each sentence
using the words given.**

1. It's a stressful city.

   It isn't a relaxing city.   (not relaxing)

2. The streets are always full of people.

   _____   (crowded)

3. It's not a very beautiful city.

   _____   (fairly ugly)

4. When should we visit the city?

   _____   (a good time)

5. You really should visit the weekend market.

   _____   (not miss)

12 It really works!

1 **Any suggestions?**

A Check (✓) the best advice for each health problem.

1. **a backache**
   - ✓ use a heating pad
   - ☐ get some exercise
   - ☐ drink herbal tea

2. **a headache**
   - ☐ take some vitamin C
   - ☐ take some aspirin
   - ☐ take a cough drop

3. **a bad cold**
   - ☐ see a dentist
   - ☐ go to bed and rest
   - ☐ go swimming

4. **an insect bite**
   - ☐ apply anti-itch cream
   - ☐ use eye drops
   - ☐ drink lots of liquids

5. **sore muscles**
   - ☐ drink lots of hot water
   - ☐ take some cold medicine
   - ☐ use some ointment

6. **a burn**
   - ☐ take a multivitamin
   - ☐ put it under cold water
   - ☐ drink warm milk

B Write a question about each problem in part A. Then write answers using the words from the box. Use the advice in part A or your own ideas.

It's important . . .   It's helpful . . .   It's a good idea . . .

1. A: _What should you do for a backache?_
   B: _It's helpful to use a heating pad._

2. A: _____
   B: _____

3. A: _____
   B: _____

4. A: _____
   B: _____

5. A: _____
   B: _____

6. A: _____
   B: _____

2 *Rewrite these sentences. Find another way to give advice using It's important . . . , It's a good idea . . . , or It's helpful . . . .*

> ### Grammar note: Negative infinitives
>
> | **Problem** | **Advice** | **Negative infinitive** |
> |---|---|---|
> | For the flu, | don't exercise a lot. | For the flu, it's a good idea **not to exercise** a lot. |

1. For a toothache, don't eat cold foods.

   For a toothache, it's important not to eat cold foods.

2. For a sore throat, don't talk too much.

   _____

3. For a burn, don't put ice on it.

   _____

4. For insomnia, don't drink coffee at night.

   _____

5. For a fever, don't get out of bed.

   _____

3 *Check (✓) three health problems you have had. Write what you did for each one. Use the remedies below or your own remedies.*

Health problems

☐ a backache
☐ a headache
☐ a toothache
☐ a cold
☐ a sore throat
☐ the hiccups
☐ a sunburn
☐ stress

Some remedies

take some aspirin   get some medicine from the drugstore
use some lotion   put some ointment on it
take some cough drops   see my doctor/dentist
go to bed   do nothing

Example: *Yesterday, I had a bad headache so I took some aspirin.*

1. _____

2. _____

3. _____

Getting to sleep

A How many hours do you sleep each night? Do you ever have difficulty getting to sleep? What do you do? Read the article.

Sleep

Most people need seven to eight hours of sleep a night. Some people need less than this, and some people need more.

According to sleep expert Dr. Robert Schachter, many people have difficulty sleeping, but they do not know why. Most people know it is important not to drink coffee or tea before they go to bed – both beverages have caffeine. Caffeine keeps people awake. However, not everybody knows that some medicines, such as cold tablets, also have caffeine in them. Stress can cause insomnia, too. Busy people with stressful jobs may not be able to sleep at night.

Dr. Schachter suggests, "You shouldn't use your bedroom as a TV room or an exercise room. You should use it for sleeping only. It's a good idea to have a regular sleeping schedule. Get up and go to bed at the same time every day. It's also important not to eat before bedtime. Eating may keep you awake."

And if all this doesn't work, try counting sheep!

B Check (✓) True or False.

	True	False
1. Everyone needs eight hours of sleep a night.	☐	☐
2. Caffeine helps you fall asleep.	☐	☐
3. Cold tablets can keep you awake.	☐	☐
4. Busy people may have trouble falling asleep.	☐	☐
5. It is a good idea to have a TV near your bed.	☐	☐
6. You should have regular sleeping hours.	☐	☐
7. You shouldn't eat just before you go to bed.	☐	☐
8. Counting sheep may help people sleep.	☐	☐

5 *What do you suggest?*

A Complete the word map with medicines from the list.

☐ anti-itch cream ☐ cough drops ☐ eye drops ☐ muscle ointment
☐ bandages ☑ ear drops ☐ insect spray ☐ sunburn spray

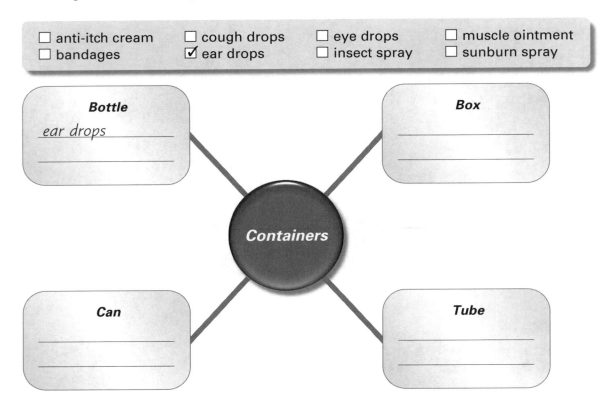

Bottle
ear drops
_____

Box
_____
_____

Containers

Can
_____
_____

Tube
_____
_____

B What should these people buy? Give advice. Use the containers and medicine from part A.

1. Joe has very tired eyes.

   He should buy a bottle of eye drops.

2. Mary has a bad cough.

   _____

3. David has a terrible earache.

   _____

4. Andrew and Carlos have a lot of mosquito bites.

   _____

5. Manuel has dry, itchy skin.

   _____

6. Susan has a cut on her hand.

   _____

7. Jin Sook and Brandy got burned at the beach.

   _____

8. Mark's shoulders are sore after his workout.

   _____

6 *Check (✓) the correct sentences to make conversations.*

1. Pharmacist: ☑ Can I help you?
   ☐ Should I help you?

   Customer: ☐ Yes. Can I have a bottle of aspirin?
   ☐ Yes. I suggest a bottle of aspirin.

   Pharmacist: Here you are.

   Customer: ☐ And what do you need for a sunburn?
   ☐ And what do you have for a sunburn?

   Pharmacist: ☐ Do you suggest this lotion?
   ☐ I suggest this lotion.

   Customer: Thanks.

2. Pharmacist: Hi. Can I help you?

   Customer: ☐ Yes. Can I suggest something for sore muscles?
   ☐ Yes. Could I have something for sore muscles?

   Pharmacist: ☐ Sure. Try this ointment.
   ☐ Sure. Could I try this ointment?

   Customer: ☐ Thanks. And what should you get for the flu?
   ☐ Thanks. And what do you suggest for the flu?

   Pharmacist: ☐ Can I have some of these tablets? They really work.
   ☐ Try some of these tablets. They really work.

   Customer: ☐ OK, thanks. I'll take them. And you should get a pack of tissues.
   ☐ OK, thanks. I'll take them. And could I have a pack of tissues?

   Pharmacist: Sure. Here you are.

7 *Complete this conversation with the correct words.*

A: Wow, you don't look very good! Do you feel OK?

B: No, I think I'm getting a cold. What should I do _____ it?
                                          (for / to / with)

A: You should stay _____ home and go _____ bed.
                  (at / in / of)   (in / of / to)

B: You're probably right. I've got a really bad cough, too.

A: Try drinking some hot tea _____ honey. It really helps.
                        (for / of / with)

B: Anything else?

A: Yeah, I suggest you get a big box _____ tissues!
                              (at / in / of)

8 *Give suggestions for these problems. Use words from the box.*

> Try . . .   I suggest . . .   You should . . .

1. I have a very sore throat.
   Try some hot tea.

2. I think I'm getting a cold.
   _____

3. I can't stop sneezing.
   _____

4. I don't have any energy.
   _____

5. I'm stressed out!
   _____

13 May I take your order?

1 *Show that you agree. Write sentences with the words given.*

1. A: I don't want fast food tonight.

   B: _I don't either._____ (either)

2. A: I really like healthy foods.

   B: _____ (so)

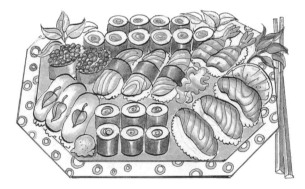

3. A: I'm in the mood for Japanese food.

   B: _____ (too)

4. A: I can't stand spicy food.

   B: _____ (neither)

5. A: I don't like bland food very much.

   B: _____ (either)

6. A: I think Italian food is delicious.

   B: _____ (too)

A Look at the pictures. Write sentences about the food.
Use the expressions in the box and the given words.

useful expressions

I love . . .   I'm not crazy about . . .
I'm crazy about . . .   I don't like . . . very much.
I like . . . a lot.   I can't stand . . .
It's a little too . . .

greasy

1. *It's a little too greasy.*

healthy

2. _____

salty

3. _____

bland

4. _____

rich

5. _____

B What are your three favorite kinds of food? Write about why you like them.

_____
_____
_____
_____

A What kinds of restaurants do you like? Do you prefer a quiet place or a noisy place? What's important to you when choosing a restaurant?

B Read these restaurant reviews.

★★★★

Trattoria Romana is an excellent Italian restaurant. It has a quiet and relaxing atmosphere, and the service is very good. It's always crowded, so make a reservation early. The menu is not very big. There are only four entrées on the menu, but everything is fresh. The chicken with pasta is wonderful. Desserts are their specialty – rich and really delicious! It's a little expensive but very good. You'll spend about $25 per person.

★★

Last Saturday, I was the only customer at ***Dynasty***, a new diner on 57th Street. It's not a good place to go. The waiters are slow and unfriendly. The atmosphere is boring, and so is the menu. The restaurant specializes in American food – mostly steak and potatoes, but my steak was raw and the fries were greasy. It isn't cheap, either. It cost me $22. If you go there, you certainly won't need a reservation. My advice, however, is clear and simple: "Don't go!"

★★★

Beirut Café is a great new Lebanese restaurant located downtown on the corner of 12th and Maple. The specialty is *meze* – lots of different small dishes, some with meat or fish, and others with vegetables. The atmosphere is lively, and the service is very friendly. There's live Lebanese music and dancing on weekends. Beirut Café is surprisingly inexpensive – about $18 a person, but you need to make a reservation. Check it out next time you're downtown.

C Complete the chart.

	Trattoria Romana	Dynasty	Beirut Café
Food	*Italian*		
Atmosphere	*quiet and relaxing*		
Specialties			
Service			
Price/person			
Reservation	☐ yes ☐ no	☐ yes ☐ no	☐ yes ☐ no

4 Check (✓) the item that does not belong.

1. ☐ iced tea
   ☑ chicken kebabs
   ☐ ice cream

2. ☐ seafood salad
   ☐ roasted lamb
   ☐ shrimp curry

3. ☐ beef burrito
   ☐ mushroom pizza
   ☐ cheese omelet

4. ☐ mashed potatoes
   ☐ french fries
   ☐ garlic bread

5. ☐ popcorn
   ☐ grilled salmon
   ☐ potato chips

6. ☐ sushi
   ☐ iced coffee
   ☐ hot chocolate

5 Use one or more words to complete this conversation between a waiter and a customer.

Waiter: May I take your order?

Customer: _Yes, I'll have_ the roast beef with mashed potatoes.

Waiter: What kind of dressing _____ on your salad – French, Italian, or vinaigrette?

Customer: _____ like French, please.

Waiter: And would you like _____ to drink?

Customer: Yes, _____ have iced coffee.

Waiter: With milk and sugar?

Customer: Yes, _____ .

Waiter: Anything else?

Customer: No, _____ . That'll _____ all.

Waiter: OK. I'll bring it right away.

6 Choose the correct responses.

1. A: Would you like fries or cole slaw?

   B: *I'll have the cole slaw, please.*

   - I guess I will, thanks.
   - I'll have the cole slaw, please.
   - Yes, please.

2. A: What kind of soda would you like?

   B: _____

   - I'll have a cola.
   - I'd like a hot dog, please.
   - A small order, please.

3. A: Would you like anything to drink?

   B: _____

   - No, thanks.
   - Yes, a hamburger, please.
   - I'll have chocolate cake, please.

4. A: What flavor ice cream would you like?

   B: _____

   - Baked, please.
   - Vanilla, please.
   - Ice cream, please.

5. A: Would you like anything else?

   B: _____

   - Yes, thank you very much.
   - Not at all, thanks.
   - That will be all, thanks.

7 Complete the conversation. Use the words and expressions in the box.

☐ am	☑ neither	☐ will	☐ can't stand them
☐ can	☐ so	☐ would	☐ favorite kind of food
☐ do	☐ too	☐ like it a lot	

Sherry: I feel tired tonight. I really don't want to cook.

Whitney: _____*Neither*_____ do I. Say, do you like Thai food?

Sherry: It's delicious! I _____ !

Whitney: I do, _____ . It's my _____ .

　　　　 Let's call Chiang Mai restaurant for home delivery.

Sherry: Great idea! Their food is always good. I eat there a lot.

Whitney: _____ do I. Well, what _____ you like tonight?

Sherry: I'm in the mood for some soup.

Whitney: So _____ I. And I think I _____ have spicy

　　　　 chicken and special Thai rice.

Sherry: OK, let's order. Oh, wait a minute, I don't have any money with me.

Whitney: Neither _____ I. What should we do?

Sherry: Well, let's look in the refrigerator. Hmm. Do you like boiled eggs?

Whitney: I _____ !

Sherry: Actually, neither _____ I.

8 Choose the correct words.

1. In a restaurant, the waiter or waitress takes your _____*order*_____ . (menu / order / service)

2. Baked potatoes are less _____ than french fries. (greasy / healthy / spicy)

3. Many people like _____ on their salad. (dessert / dressing / soda)

4. Some people rarely cook with spices. They prefer _____ food. (bland / hot / rich)

5. Vanilla is a popular ice cream _____ . (drink / flavor / meal)

14 The biggest and the best!

1 Geography

A Circle the correct word.

1. This is a stream of water occurring when a river falls from a high place.
   a. waterfall   b. ocean   c. hill

2. This is a large area of land that has lots of trees on it.
   a. desert   b. forest   c. river

3. This is a low area of land between mountains or hills.
   a. valley   b. river   c. beach

4. This is an area of water with land all around it.
   a. lake   b. ocean   c. island

5. This is a mountain with a hole on top. Smoke and lava sometimes come out, and it can be dangerous.
   a. hill   b. canyon   c. volcano

6. This is a dry, sandy place. It doesn't rain much here, and there aren't many plants.
   a. desert   b. sea   c. volcano

B Complete the names. Use words from the box.

☑ Canyon   ☐ Falls   ☐ Ocean   ☐ Lake
☐ Desert   ☐ Mount   ☐ River   ☐ Sea

1. Grand _Canyon_
2. Amazon _____
3. _____ Superior
4. _____ Fuji
5. Mediterranean _____
6. Angel _____
7. Pacific _____
8. Sahara _____

79

2 *Write the comparative and superlative of the words given.*

Spelling note: Comparatives and superlatives

	Adjective	Comparative	Superlative
Add **-er** or **-est** *to most words.*	long	long**er**	the long**est**
Add **-r** or **-st** *to words ending in* **-e.**	large	larg**er**	the larg**est**
Drop **y** *and add* **-ier** *or* **-iest.**	dry	dri**er**	the dri**est**
Double the final consonant and add **-er** *or* **-est.**	big	bigg**er**	the bigg**est**

1. busy   *busier*   *the busiest*

2. cool   _____   _____

3. friendly _____   _____

4. heavy   _____   _____

5. nice   _____   _____

6. noisy   _____   _____

7. old   _____   _____

8. safe   _____   _____

9. small   _____   _____

10. wet   _____   _____

3 *Complete this conversation.*
Use the superlative of the words given.

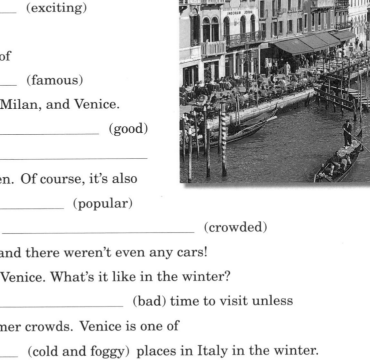

the Grand Canal

Ian: So where did you go for your vacation, Val?

Val: Italy.

Ian: How exciting! Did you have a good time?

Val: It was terrific! I think Italy is

   *the most exciting*_____ (exciting)

   country in Europe.

Ian: Well, it certainly has some of

   _____ (famous)

   cities in the world – Rome, Milan, and Venice.

Val: Yeah. I had _____ (good)

   time in Venice. It's _____

   (beautiful) city I've ever seen. Of course, it's also

   one of _____ (popular)

   tourist attractions. It was _____ (crowded)

   city I visited this summer, and there weren't even any cars!

Ian: I've always wanted to visit Venice. What's it like in the winter?

Val: Actually, that's _____ (bad) time to visit unless

   you want to avoid the summer crowds. Venice is one of

   _____ (cold and foggy) places in Italy in the winter.

4 Complete these sentences. Use the comparative or the superlative of the words given.

the Suez Canal, Egypt

Mount Waialeale, USA

Death Valley, USA

1. Canada and Russia are _____ *the largest* _____ (large) countries in the world.

2. Russia is _____ *larger than* _____ (large) Canada.

3. _____ (high) waterfall in the world is in Venezuela.

4. The Suez Canal joins the Mediterranean and Red seas. It is 190 kilometers (118 miles)

   long. It is _____ (long) the Panama Canal.

5. The Atacama Desert in Chile is _____ (dry) place in the world.

6. Mount Waialeale in Hawaii gets 1,170 centimeters (460 inches) of rain a year.

   It is _____ (wet) place on earth!

7. _____ (hot) capital city in the world is Muscat, in Oman.

8. The continent of Antarctica is _____ (cold) any other place

   in the world.

9. The Himalayas are some of _____ (dangerous) mountains to climb.

10. Badwater, in California's Death Valley, is _____ (low) point

    in North America.

11. Mont Blanc in the French Alps is _____ (high) the Matterhorn

    in the Swiss Alps.

12. The Pacific Ocean is _____ (deep) the Atlantic Ocean.

    At one place the Pacific Ocean is 11,033 meters (36,198 feet) deep.

5 *The coldest and the windiest!*

A Where is the coldest place you've ever been?

B Read about Antarctica.

ANTARCTICA is the most southern continent in the world. It's like nowhere else on earth. It's much larger than Europe and nearly twice the size of Australia. It's an icy plateau with the South Pole at its center. Antarctica is the coldest and windiest place in the world, even colder and windier than the North Pole. In the summer, the sun shines for 24 hours a day, but in the winter it's completely dark for about three months. Very few plants grow there, but there is some wildlife, including whales, seals, and penguins.

When Captain James Cook sailed around the continent in the 1770s, he found no one living there. Today, a few scientists work in Antarctica, but they only spend fairly short periods there. Many of the scientists in Antarctica are studying the ozone layer. The ozone layer is getting thinner and thinner worldwide. The biggest "hole" is over Antarctica, where the weather is getting warmer. Scientists think that this cold and lonely place can teach us a lot about the earth and how to keep it safe.

C Check (✓) True or False.

	True	False
1. Europe is bigger than Antarctica.	☐	☐
2. The North Pole is the coldest and windiest place in the world.	☐	☐
3. In Antarctica, it never gets dark in the summer.	☐	☐
4. There are a lot of animals and birds in Antarctica.	☐	☐
5. Captain Cook found a few scientists living in Antarctica.	☐	☐
6. The weather in Antarctica is getting colder and colder.	☐	☐

Use the words in the box. Write questions about the pictures.
Then circle the correct answers.

☐ How big	☐ How deep	☐ How long
☐ How cold	☐ How far	☑ How high

Angel Falls

1. _How high is Angel Falls?_
   a. It's 979 meters (3,212 feet) tall.
   b. It's 979 meters high.

Australia to New Zealand

Australia

New Zealand

2. _____
   a. It's about 2,000 kilometers (1,200 miles).
   b. It's about 2,000 square kilometers.

the Amazon River

3. _____
   a. It's 6,437 kilometers (4,000 miles) long.
   b. It's 6,437 kilometers high.

Antarctica

4. _____
   a. It gets up to –88.3 degrees Celsius
      (–126.9 degrees Fahrenheit).
   b. It gets down to –88.3 degrees Celsius.

the Amazon Rain Forest

5. _____
   a. It's 6 million square kilometers (2.5 million miles).
   b. It's 6 million kilometers long.

the Grand Canyon

6. _____
   a. It's about 1.6 kilometers (1 mile) big.
   b. It's about 1.6 kilometers deep.

7 Answer these questions about your home country.

1. How big is the largest city?
   _____

2. What's the wettest month?
   _____

3. What's the driest month?
   _____

4. How hot does it get in the summer?
   _____

5. How cold does it get in the winter?
   _____

6. How far is the nearest beach?
   _____

7. How high is the highest mountain?
   _____

8. What's the most beautiful town to visit?
   _____

8 Write the opposites to complete the crossword puzzle.

Across

2 biggest
6 bad
7 shorter
8 worse
9 worst
10 near
11 lowest
13 driest
14 hot
15 shortest

Down

1 hotter
3 smaller
4 least crowded
   (2 words)
5 coldest
9 smallest
10 not famous
11 cold
12 best

84 • Unit 14

15 I'm going to a soccer match.

1 **Match the words in columns A and B. Write the names of the activities.**
(More than one answer may be possible.)

A	B	
☑ birthday	☐ act	1. _birthday party_
☐ comedy	☐ concert	2. _____
☐ dance	☐ fair	3. _____
☐ golf	☐ game	4. _____
☐ pop	☐ match	5. _____
☐ soccer	☑ party	6. _____
☐ street	☐ performance	7. _____
☐ volleyball	☐ tournament	8. _____

2 **Read Anna's diary, and write about her plans. Use the present continuous.**

July

Sunday	Monday	Tuesday	Wednesday	Thursday	Friday	Saturday
6	7	8	9	10	11	12
afternoon – go to Jeremy's birthday party	work overtime to finish the report	7:00 P.M. – see a play with Tony	night – watch the tennis match with Kate & Sam	12:00 noon – have lunch with Candy	stay home and watch the baseball game on TV	afternoon – go to the golf tournament

1. _On Sunday afternoon, Anna is going to Jeremy's birthday party._
2. _____
3. _____
4. _____
5. _____
6. _____
7. _____

3 Complete this conversation. Use **be going to**
and the verbs given.

Marta: What ___are___ you ___going to do___ this weekend, Mark? (do)

Mark: I _____ to a rock concert on Saturday. (go)

Marta: That sounds interesting.

Mark: Yeah. There's a free concert in the park. And how about you, Marta?

Marta: Well, Brian and I _____ a basketball game

    in the afternoon. (see)

Mark: And what _____ you _____ in the evening? (do)

Marta: Brian _____ his mother in the hospital. (visit)

    But I _____ not _____ anything really. (do)

Mark: Well, I _____ some friends over

    for a barbecue. Would you like to come? (have)

Marta: Thanks. I'd love to!

4 Choose the correct responses.

1. A: Would you like to have dinner at Rosa's tonight?

   B: _Great! But it's my turn to pay._

    ■ No, I'm not doing anything.
    ■ Sorry, I'm going away next week.
    ■ Great! But it's my turn to pay.

2. A: Do you want to visit the street fair with us tomorrow?

   B: _____

    ■ Yes, I'm going to.
    ■ Can we go to a late show?
    ■ Sure, I'd love to.

3. A: We're having friends over for dinner tonight.
    Would you like to come?

   B: _____

    ■ How about this evening?
    ■ I'm sorry. I'm working late tonight.
    ■ Yes, it would.

4. A: How about going to a movie on Saturday?

   B: _____

    ■ Oh, I'm sorry. I can't.
    ■ Nothing special.
    ■ No. I wouldn't.

5 Write invitations to this week's events in Princeville.

Exciting things to do this week in Princeville All events scheduled to begin at 8:00 P.M.

Wednesday	Thursday	Friday	Saturday
Rock concert U2	**Amusement park** Lots to do for everyone!	**Musical** *The Lion King*	**Museum** Exhibition of modern art

1. *Are you doing anything on Wednesday evening? Do you want to see a rock concert?*
   OR *I'm going to see U2 on Wednesday. Would you like to come?*

2. _____

3. _____

4. _____

6 Write about how often you do these leisure activities. Use the expressions in the box.

I often . . .
I . . . almost every weekend.
I sometimes . . . in the summer.
I . . . three or four times a year.
I never . . .

1. _____
2. _____
3. _____
4. _____
5. _____
6. _____

1. go to rock concerts
2. go for long walks
3. have parties at home
4. see plays
5. visit amusement parks
6. watch ballgames

I'm going to a soccer match. • 87

A Have you ever sent or received text messages? Now read about them.

TEXT MESSAGES — *here to stay*

Text messages are short, typed messages of 150 characters each. The messages can include letters, numbers, and spaces. They are sent by Short Message Services, or SMS. This technology allows users to send and receive text messages on their cell phones. People can also send text messages from computers to a cell phone, and vice versa. This new way of communicating can save both time and money. And it's a lot of fun!

Text messages use a kind of "text talk" language. Words in text messages are often spelled the way they sound. For example, "Talk to you later" becomes "TLK2UL8R." When you abbreviate your words in this way, you can write messages faster. And you can fit more words into a short message on a small cell phone screen.

Text messages often contain emoticons. You can create these icons or small pictures with your keyboard. It's easier to understand them vertically, so turn your head to the left to look at these examples:

Incoming Message >>

B *I* U

TLK2UL8R

:-) equals "happy/smile"   ;-D equals "wink + big smile"   :-(equals "sad"

You can see this new electronic language in Internet chat rooms and in instant messaging. Have you ever received a text message but didn't know what it meant? Were you confused? Well, you're not alone. The more you use this new way to communicate, the better and faster you'll become at it. B4N (Bye for now) and BOL (Best of luck)!

B Can you guess what these text messages mean? Match each one with its meaning.

1. BBL	*h*	a.	I see.
2. ILBL8	___	b.	Where are you from?
3. CU	___	c.	Laughing out loud.
4. SUP	___	d.	Please.
5. ILY	___	e.	I'll be late.
6. WUF?	___	f.	See you.
7. IC	___	g.	Thanks.
8. THX	___	✓h.	Be back later.
9. LOL	___	i.	What's up?
10. PLZ	___	j.	I love you.

8 *Read these messages. What did the caller say?*
Write the messages another way using **tell or ask.**

For:	Ms. Tam
Message:	The meeting is at 10:30. Bring the fax from New York.

1. *Please tell Ms. Tam that the meeting is at 10:30.*
   Could you . . .

For:	Mr. Alvarez
Message:	We need the report by noon. Call Ms. James as soon as possible.

2. _____

For:	Miss Lowe
Message:	The new laptop is ready. Pick it up this afternoon.

3. _____

9 *Look at the message slips. Ask someone to give these messages.*

> ### Grammar note: Negative infinitives
>
> | **Request** | **Message** |
> |-------------|-------------|
> | **Don't call** him today. | Please ask Jan **not to call** him today. |
> | **Don't go** home yet. | Could you tell him **not to go** home yet? |

Michael -
Don't meet me at the airport
until midnight. The plane is going
to be late.

1. _____

Lucy -
We're meeting at Dino's house before
the concert. Don't forget the tickets.

2. _____

Christopher—
The beach party starts at noon.
Don't be late!

3. _____

10 **Choose the correct words.**

Secretary: Hello. Schmidt and Lee.

Ms. Curtis: _May I_ _____ speak to Ms. Grace Schmidt, please?
(May I / Would you)

Secretary: I'm _____. She's not in. _____
(busy / sorry) (Can I leave / Can I take)

a messsage?

Ms. Curtis: Yes, please. This is Ms. Curtis. _____ you
(Would / Please)

_____ I'm staying at the Plaza Hotel?
(tell her that / ask her to)

The number is 555-9001, Room 605. _____
(Please / Could)

you _____ ?
(tell her to call me / tell her to call her)

Secretary: OK, Ms. Curtis. I'll _____
(give her / tell her)

the messsage.

Ms. Curtis: Thank you very much. Good-bye.

11 **Match the questions with the correct responses.**

☐ Yes, please. Could you tell him Roz called?	☐ Let me see if he's in.
☐ That's OK. I'll call back.	☐ My name's Graham. Graham Lock.
☐ Yes. My number is (303) 555-3241.	☑ Yes, that would be great. Thanks.

1. Would you like to come to a party?
   Yes, that would be great. Thanks.

2. Could I ask her to call you back?
   _____

3. Who's calling?
   _____

4. Can I take a message?
   _____

5. Could I speak to Paul, please?
   _____

6. I'm sorry. She's busy at the moment.
   _____

16 A change for the better!

1 Choose the correct responses.

1. A: Say, you really look different.

   B: _Well, my hair is a little longer now._

   - I moved into a new house.
   - I'm more outgoing than before.
   - Well, my hair is a little longer now.

2. A: I haven't seen you for ages.

   B: _____

   - I know. How have you been?
   - Well, I got a bank loan.
   - My new job is more stressful.

3. A: You know, I have three kids now.

   B: _____

   - Well, I've grown a mustache.
   - That's terrific!
   - Say, you've really changed your hair.

4. A: How are you?

   B: _____

   - I do more aerobics these days.
   - Well, actually, I turned 18.
   - I'm doing really well.

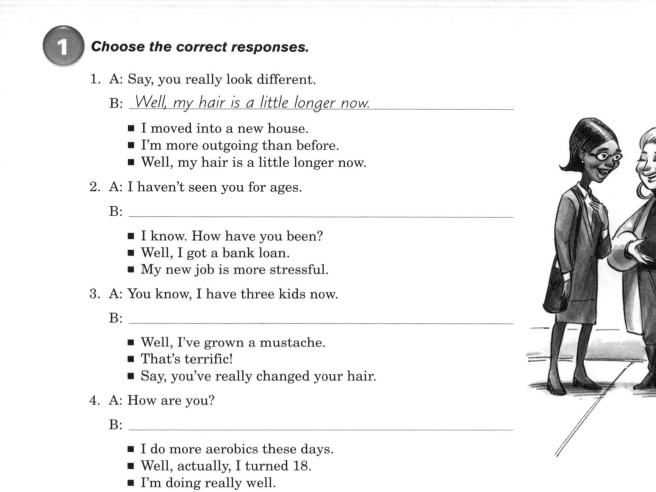

2 Complete the sentences. Use information in the box and the present perfect.

□ move to a new apartment   □ start going to the gym   □ stop eating in restaurants

1. Judy _____ .

   Her old one was too small.

2. Kim and Anna _____ .

   Now they cook dinner at home every evening. It's much cheaper.

3. Alex _____ .

   He looks healthier, and he has more energy.

3 Describe how these people have changed. Use the present or the past tense.

Shawn

1. _Shawn grew a lot._

Elena

2. _____

Susan

3. _____

Eddie

4. _____

4 Rewrite these sentences. Find another way to say each sentence using the words given.

1. Alice quit eating rich food.

   Alice eats healthier food now. (healthier)

2. James lost a lot of weight.

   _____ (heavier)

3. Mary goes to a new school now.

   _____ (change)

4. Tess got divorced last year.

   _____ (married)

5. I've grown out my hair.

   _____ (longer)

6. We don't work out anymore.

   _____ (quit)

A Have you ever . . . ?

- ☐ lost a job
- ☐ had money problems
- ☐ had trouble making friends
- ☐ worked in a foreign country

B Read the passages on the left. Then read the passages on the right. Match the people's lives two years ago with their lives today.

Aki

Luis and his wife

Rosie

Two years ago	Now
1. **Aki** Two years ago, I was a student, and I thought life was really good. I got up late. I spent the day talking to friends, and then I studied all night. I wore jeans and sweatshirts and had long hair and a mustache. I felt free. _____	a. Now my life has completely changed. I got married six months ago! My wife and I often have friends over for dinner. We're taking classes several nights a week. It's great! We're even talking about starting a family soon.
2. **Luis** I moved to a new town two years ago. My job was interesting, but I was single and I didn't have any friends. People at work were friendly but not very outgoing. We never did anything after work. _____	b. Now I work as a computer programmer for an international company. I've moved to Seoul and have started to learn Korean. Korean food is great, and I've gained several kilos. I feel much happier and healthier.
3. **Rosie** My life seemed to come to an end two years ago. I lost my job. Then I lost weight, and looked terrible. Money became a problem. I was very sad. I needed some good luck. _____	c. Now I actually look forward to getting up early in the morning and going to work. Of course, I dress up now, and my hair is shorter. But I don't really mind. At least my evenings are free!

C Underline at least two changes in each person's life.

6 Complete the sentences. Use words in the box.

☐ broke   ☑ graduation   ☐ responsibilities
☐ career   ☐ loan   ☐ successful

1. After _____ *graduation* _____ , Kirk and Nancy plan to look for jobs.

2. What _____ do you think you're most interested in pursuing?

3. I go to school, and I have a family and a part-time job. I have a lot of _____ .

4. Lucy wants to pay off her student _____ before she buys a car.

5. Marie lost her job. Now she's _____ , and she can't pay her rent.

6. I'd like to be _____ in my first job. Then I can get a better job and a raise.

7 Complete this conversation. Use the words given.

Melissa: What _do you plan to do_____ (plan, do) this summer, Leo?

Leo: I _____ (want, get) a summer job.

I _____ (like, save) money for a vacation.

Melissa: Really? Where _____ (like, go) ?

Leo: I _____ (love, travel) to Latin America. What about you, Melissa?

Melissa: Well, I _____ (not go, get) a job right away.

First, I _____ (want, go) to Spain and Portugal.

Leo: Sounds great, but how _____ (go, pay) for it?

Melissa: I _____ (hope, borrow) some money from my brother. I have a good excuse. I _____ (plan, take) courses in Spanish and Portuguese.

Leo: Oh, I'm tired of studying!

Melissa: So am I. But I also _____ (hope, take) people on tours to Latin America. Why don't you come on my first tour?

Leo: Count me in!

8

Imagine you have these problems. Write three sentences about changing each situation. Use words in the box.

1. I'm not interested in my job these days. I spend three hours driving to and from work every day, and I don't make enough money! I can't find a new job, though, because of my poor computer skills.

    | I hope to . . .   I want to . . .   I plan to . . . |

    _____

    _____

    _____

2. I've become less careful about my health lately. I've stopped jogging because I'm bored with it. I've started eating more fast food because I'm too tired to cook after work. And I can't sleep at night.

    | I'm going to . . .   I'd like to . . .   I'd love to . . . |

    _____

    _____

    _____

3. I just moved to a new town, and I don't know anyone. I never do anything after work. People at work don't really talk to me. I haven't had a date in about four months. And I never seem to do anything fun in the evenings.

    | I'm going to . . .   I want to . . .   I plan to . . . |

    _____

    _____

    _____

9

Choose the correct words to complete each sentence. Use the correct form of the word or add any words necessary.

1. I need _____*to get*_____ a bank loan. I hope to buy a
   (open / start / get)

   house soon.

2. Heather's salary is much _____ before.
   (low / short / high)

   She had to take a pay cut.

3. After graduation, Jack plans _____ for an
   (play / work / move)

   international company.

4. This job is _____ my last job.
   (outgoing / stressful / expensive)

5. Mel hopes _____ to a small town.
   (move / live / change)

6. William and Donna got _____ last
   (engage / marry / divorce)

   summer. The marriage will be in April.

10

Advise people how to make changes in their lives. Use expressions like the ones in the box.

> You should . . .   You shouldn't . . .   Why don't you . . .

1. I've gained a lot of weight this year.

   _____

2. My hair is longer, but it doesn't look good.

   _____

3. I've gotten tired of wearing the same old clothes.

   _____

4. I want to start a successful business.

   _____

5. I'm often bored on weekends.

   _____

6. I don't seem to have any goals.

   _____

7. I've finished this textbook, but I still want to improve my English!

   _____